Qualifications in the UK

How to make the right choices

Toby Higson

RIVINGTON

QUALIFICATIONS IN THE UK
How to make the right choices
www.qualificationconsumer.com

© Rivington Publishing 2011

First published in Great Britain in 2011 by
RIVINGTON PUBLISHING LIMITED
2nd Floor, 145-157 St John Street
London EC1V 4PY
www.rivingtonbooks.com

All rights reserved

No part of this publication may be reproduced, stored in a retrieval system or transmitted in any form or by any means including photocopying, electronic, mechanical, recording or otherwise, without prior written permission from the Publishers. All trade marks used in this publication are the property of their respective owners.

A CIP catalogue record of this book is available from the British Library

ISBN 978-1-8457-8020-3

Toby Higson asserts the moral right to be identified as the author of this work

The cases and examples used in this publication are included purely as illustrations. No endorsement or criticism of any organisation or individual manager is intended or should be inferred.

Cover design by Tom Lynton
Printed and bound in Great Britain by Bell & Bain, Glasgow

Contents

Introduction	1
The value of this book	2
A guide to the book	2
Annexes	5
Chapter 1 – Some fundamentals	7
What is a qualification?	8
The qualification 'standard'	9
The importance of reputation	9
How qualifications are structured	10
Learning outcomes	12
The importance of good titling	13
The length of a qualification	14
Credit	15
Transferring learning with credit	16
Assessment	18
How do you like to learn?	21
Some vocabulary	22
Chapter 2 – The qualification system in the UK	25
Why the qualification system in the UK can be so confusing	26
The free market in qualifications	27
Qualification developers	27
Quality assurance	30
The delivery of qualifications	32
Chapter 3 – How to choose the right level of qualification	37
The significance of 'level'	38
Getting the right information from a complex system	40

Chapter 4 – How to judge the cost of a qualification   43
    The cost of a qualification   44
    Quality indicators   49
    Funding   50

Chapter 5 – How to judge the quality of a qualification   57
    Good information   58
    Certification   61
    Regulated and quality-assured   62
    Reputation and employability   66
    Quality indicators   68

Chapter 6 – How to judge the quality of assessment   71
    What do you need to know about assessment?   72
    Assessment that is fair and accurate   78
    How your questions and issues on assessment should be managed   84
    Quality indicators   85

Chapter 7 – How to judge the quality of a learning provider   87
    Robust entry requirements and application procedures   88
    The quality of the information provided by the learning provider   90
    The quality of resources and learning environment   94
    The quality of teaching and support provided by a learning provider   98
    The quality of service provided to disabled learners   100
    Customer services and the management of complaints   102
    The management of poor practice   103
    How to utilise inspection reports and other sources of information on the quality of learning providers   105
    Quality indicators   111

Chapter 8 – How to get information and advice   113
    Where to search for the right qualification   114
    Help and advice   117
    Where to go to get help and advice as an international student   121
    Where to get help and advice as a disabled learner   121

Chapter 9 – Going abroad with your qualification   123
    'Qualifications can cross boundaries'   125
    The European Qualifications Framework (EQF)   126
    Other useful tools and sources of information   128

Chapter 10 – Your rights as a qualification consumer   133
    Who is accountable for your qualification   134
    Your fundamental rights as a qualification consumer   135
    The right to good customer service   136
    The right to teaching of high quality   137
    The right to a well-resourced learning environment   138
    The right not to be discriminated against   139
    The right to be charged a fair price   140
    The right for your qualification to be clearly described   141
    The right to be confident in the standard of your qualification   143
    The right to reliable and fair assessment practices   143
    The right to have your work remarked or resit your examination   145
    The right to complain   146
    The right for your personal information to be managed securely   146
    The right to receive a uniquely identifiable qualification certificate   147
    The rational consumer   148

Annex 1 – The qualification frameworks in the UK   151
    The significance of the different qualification 'levels'   152

Annex 2 – An overview of the types of learning provider in the UK   159
    Compulsory education up to 16   159
    Post-16 education   161
    Higher education and adult learning   161

Annex 3 – An overview of the types of qualifications available in the UK   165
    14-19 qualifications   165
    Skills-based qualifications   168
    Vocational qualifications   170
    Bachelors degrees, masters degrees and doctorates   172

Annex 4 – An overview of organisations involved in UK qualifications 175
Government departments in education 175
Qualification regulators and quality assurance agencies 176
Inspectorates and accreditation bodies 177
Organisations involved specifically in the management of complaints and appeals 178
Organisations involved in funding qualifications 178
Organisations involved in the development of skills 180
Where to search for qualifications, learning providers and get careers advice 181
Government services 181
Private organisations 184
Representative bodies 185
Help and advice for international students 185
European information services and initiatives 186
Services supporting disabled learners 187
Organisations responsible for the processing of student applications 188

Glossary 189

Index 203

Introduction

Taking a qualification can change your life by giving you the skills and confidence to move in a different direction. It can have significant implications for how much you can earn and what you will achieve. Taking a qualification is a serious commitment and frequently requires a large investment of time and money. So choosing the right qualification is very important. However, the qualifications system is complex and choosing a qualification can be daunting at any age or stage in life. There are thousands of different qualifications available, developed and delivered by a great variety of organisations.

You could compare the experience of choosing a qualification to shopping in a supermarket. The first task in the supermarket is to find the aisle where all the different brands of, say, breakfast cereal are displayed. This is easy to do. Faced with ten different brands of breakfast cereal, it could be difficult to make a choice but, again, a good supermarket clearly labels the products on its shelves so you can easily compare the contents and price.

When shopping for a qualification, all of this information is much more difficult to find. There may be ten different qualifications in hairdressing, all at the same level but provided by different organisations. The first challenge is just tracking the competing qualifications down; they will not be sitting neatly next to each other on a supermarket shelf. The bigger challenge is then to do an objective comparison of the qualifications in terms of content, quality and cost.

If we buy the wrong packet of breakfast cereal we can make sure to avoid that one next week – but a qualification is a big purchase. When we buy a TV or a car, we usually do background research – we might visit a number of stores or dealers to compare price and quality, and talk to some sales assistants, and we will probably search online.

At the moment, the qualifications industry provides nothing like the information that we get in a decent supermarket. And as qualification consumers we display nothing like the self-confidence and assertiveness that we display when we are buying a TV or a car, or that we display later when we find a problem with them.

It is important that as a consumer of qualifications you make calculated, rational decisions. It is vital that you don't let a lack of self-confidence deter you from asking searching questions. It takes time and energy to gather the information to judge which qualification is right for your needs – what level of difficulty is appropriate, what the differences are between qualifications, what constitutes value for money – and to assess the merits of the different providers offering to teach you the qualification.

The value of this book

- This book shows you how to be a rational consumer in the market for qualifications.

- The book is designed from the perspective of the consumer of qualifications.

- It explains how to make informed judgements about the quality of a qualification and about the organisation offering to teach you that qualification.

- The book explains what learners have the right to expect as they progress through their study, and what to do if something goes wrong.

- The small things matter. This book understands that small, practical considerations can have a significant bearing on the quality of a learning experience.

A guide to the book

Each chapter of this book is designed to cut through the complexity of the qualifications system in order to present the information you need in a clear and straightforward way. The book guides you towards useful resources – people to talk to, sources of information and examples of best practice.

Each chapter focuses on a particular subject and you can either read the book from start to finish, or go directly to the chapter which answers your particular needs. Here are some of the most important questions, together with the chapters that address them.

What type of qualification will suit your individual learning style?
It is worth considering what type of qualification best suits your preferred learning style. For example do you like the pressure of an end-of-course exam or do your prefer being assessed as you go along, through written assignments? What degree of flexibility do you want while learning? Do you want to learn in your own time or would you prefer learning in a classroom or workshop? Chapters 1 and 2 develop these issues. You should also go to Annexes 2 and 3 which outline the different types of learning providers and qualifications in the UK.

How important is reputation?
There are a number of questions to consider here. What is the reputation of the organisation that develops and delivers the qualification? What is the reputation of the qualification itself? You need to establish if the qualification is accepted and valued by employers or by further and higher education providers. Chapters 1, 5 and 7 discuss reputation.

What level of qualification should you take?
It is vital to get this decision right. Before starting a qualification you need to ask the following questions. Is the qualification at the right level for your needs? What does the qualification enable you to do? Does the qualification support entry into something else? To be able to answer these questions you also need to understand what information a national qualification level gives you. Chapters 3 and 5 and Annex 1 help you judge the level of a qualification.

How to establish the cost of qualification
It can be hard to clearly establish all the costs involved in taking a qualification. To do this effectively you need to be aware of the variety of costs you might face and also the language used to describe these costs. You also need to consider what funding is available. Do your circumstances, or the nature of the qualification, qualify you for external funding? It is also helpful to know where you can go for more information and advice in this area. Chapter 4 discusses cost, and funding.

How can you establish the quality of your qualification?
This is a central question for you as a qualification consumer. There are a number of dimensions to the quality of a qualification. You also need to consider how the quality of the qualification is checked and regulated, and whether the qualification is recognised by the education authorities. Chapter 5 explains how to judge the quality of the qualification, and discover how it is regulated.

How will you be assessed?
You need to be very clear on how you will be assessed. Knowing how your knowledge and skills will be tested and also the practical detail supporting a particular assessment is essential to your success. You also need to be confident that you will be assessed fairly and accurately. Chapter 6 explains what to look for.

How to establish the quality of the learning provider
How can you establish if the school, college or university is of high quality? Again, there are a number of dimensions to the quality of a learning provider, in terms of teaching, customer service, learning resources and learning environment. It is also important to examine inspectorate reports and consumer reviews. Chapter 7 explains how to assess the quality of the learning provider.

How can you get further information and advice?
A great deal of this book is focused on giving you the tools to judge the quality of a qualification and learning provider. However there are also very comprehensive qualification search engines and excellent sources of advice and support available in the UK. These are described in Chapter 8.

Will your qualification be recognised abroad?
There has been significant progress in recent years in allowing the recognition of qualifications between different countries. You might be considering moving abroad and be concerned about whether your qualifications will be recognised. Alternatively you might be looking to study or work in the UK and want to establish the value of your qualification. Chapter 9 explains how to discover how well your qualification will travel.

How can you assert your rights as a qualification consumer?
Though it is unlikely, things can go wrong when you take a qualification. Given the time, cost and effort involved in a qualification, and its potential impact on your future, you should not accept poor practice. You need to be clear on your rights as a qualifications consumer. You need to know what to do and who to speak to if something goes wrong or is not up to an acceptable standard. Chapter 10 explains your rights, and how to assert them.

Annexes

Annex 1 describes the main qualification frameworks in the UK, and using England as an example, outlines what each qualification level means in terms of knowledge and skills. Annex 2 provides an overview of the types of learning provider in the UK. Annex 3 reviews the main types of qualification available to learners. Annex 4 provides a comprehensive directory, including website addresses, of the organisations that can give information and advice on qualifications. A glossary of commonly used terms is provided at the end of the book.

Chapter 1
Some fundamentals

This chapter:

→ Defines a qualification and explains how it is structured

→ Outlines the importance of the qualification standard

→ Highlights the importance of clear titling

→ Explains how to make a judgement on the length of a qualification

→ Outlines the role of credit and how it benefits you

→ Explains the meaning of assessment and describes the different types of assessment

→ Emphasises the importance of knowing your own learning style

→ Describes some of the key terms used in describing qualifications

What is a qualification?

A *qualification* develops you for a particular purpose. In gaining a qualification you have acquired knowledge and skills in a subject. A qualification is more than the sum of its parts. However challenging or interesting particular topics are within a qualification, it is the role of the qualification to ensure the right content is covered. For example, an accountancy qualification should give you the knowledge and skills needed to enter into the accountancy profession. If the qualification falls short of developing these skills then it is not doing its job.

Motivations for taking a qualification are varied. You might take a qualification out of interest or for pleasure. A qualification might be central to your plan to retrain. Qualifications do not automatically qualify you for a particular profession, but they may be stepping stones towards entry into a profession or towards access to further education. For example, you probably need to take a number of qualifications to qualify fully as a lawyer or to gain entry to a particular university course.

Qualifications develop a range of knowledge and skills. A qualification in plumbing needs to develop the practical skills and competencies needed to be a plumber. It is worthless to be able to design a heating system on paper, if you are unable to use tools and fix everyday problems. However, while the emphasis might be on the development of practical skills, you still need a foundation of theory. To be an effective plumber requires a good knowledge of the types of pipes, valves, boilers and radiators that are available. However, knowledge of these different items is only valuable when it is combined to form an understanding of how to fix plumbing systems.

To gain a qualification you have to demonstrate the attainment of those skills to the organisation which 'owns' the qualification. This might not be the organisation that taught you the qualification. A school or college will often teach a qualification which has been developed by another body. It is that organisation, not the school or college, who is ultimately responsible for the *assessment* of the qualification and who will award you the qualification *certificate* if they are satisfied that you have met the required standards. This distinction matters to you as a learner and will be explained in more detail in Chapter 2.

The qualification 'standard'

A term used to describe the difficulty of a qualification is the *standard* of the qualification. This term is important to understand, and it is commonly misused. The standard of a qualification should be the same regardless of where it is taught in the country and which organisation is delivering it to you. Standards should be stable over time and should not keep changing. People taking a qualification might well get better results over time, but any long-term improvement in results should be due to advances in teaching and not due to the qualification getting easier.

If the same qualification was more difficult this year than last, then learners this year would be unfairly disadvantaged. If the qualification got easier over time then how would you, or the organisation hoping to employ you, know the true value of your qualification when compared to people with the same qualification taken at an earlier or later point in time? It is vital that the level of difficulty of a qualification remains constant for it to be trusted by employers or admission tutors.

It is the role of the education authorities in the UK to make sure that the standards of national qualifications remain fixed. The term *education authorities* is used to describe the agencies, regulators and *inspectorates* who have the responsibility for safeguarding the quality of qualifications and teaching. Annex 4 outlines the different organisations that make up the education authorities in the UK.

The importance of reputation

Reports in the media often focus on certain qualifications and suggest that standards are declining. For example there is a common perception that A levels and GCSEs have become easier to pass. In response, the education authorities have conducted a great deal of research into these qualifications. While there is not a consensus in this area, these reports paint a much more complex picture as to why pass rates have increased.

Despite these findings, the views of employers and *admission tutors* can be influenced by these debates in the media. It might be worth doing internet research to check media perceptions about the qualification you are interested in. You need to be aware of the reputation of the qualification, even if that reputation might not be justified.

You need to balance that reputation with how well the qualification meets your requirements. A qualification might have a mixed reputation in the media but fit your needs. If this is the case you will need to find a way to communicate the real value of your qualification when applying for a job or further studies. The danger is that an employer will look at your CV and decide not to interview you because of his or her opinion of your qualification, depriving you of a chance to make your case.

Other qualifications might have higher status, but require a sacrifice in terms of how well they suit you. This sacrifice might be acceptable, when weighed against the benefits brought by the reputation of the qualification. Ultimately what matters is that you are clear on your own priorities and are able to make an informed decision.

How qualifications are structured

Qualifications are made up of distinct blocks of learning which when added together make a coherent qualification. *Vocational qualifications* tend to use the term *'units'* and many university level qualifications use the term *'modules'*. For simplicity this book will use the term units.

Units are important because they are how the learning is organised. They give you a sense of progress as you work through a qualification. It is through reviewing the unit structure of a qualification that you can properly establish if it is right for your needs. The organisation developing the qualification needs to make sure each unit goes into sufficient depth and that the skills being developed are current and fit for purpose to enter a profession or progress onto further studies. This can be demanding as skills in areas such as Information Technology are constantly changing. The unit structure of a qualification also governs how you are assessed at different stages in the qualification. At the end of each unit you are typically assessed in some way to test that you have gained the necessary skills.

Achieving a unit of learning is also important if you do not fully complete a qualification. A unit is the smallest part of a qualification that allows you to gain some form of recognition, so even if you do not achieve the full qualification you usually have the right to get a certificate or at least a record of achievement providing evidence you have completed one or more units.

Some units are described as *mandatory, compulsory* or *core*, which means you have to do them if you want to get a qualification. Other units are *optional*, so you can select which units to take as part of your qualification.

Exhibit 1 An example of the unit structure of a qualification

---

Certificate in creating interiors

Mandatory units: (You have to do these units)

- D/600/3100   Health and safety when creating interiors
- H/6000/3101 Developing a design for an interior
- F/600/3106   Prepare to create an interior

Optional units: (You can select which options you would like to do)

- L/600/3108   Prepare resources and materials for creating interiors
- H/600/3115   Assembling and fitting units for interiors
- T/600/3118   Re-instate a location after assembly and placement of an interior
- M/600/3120   Survey a location for an interior
- F/600/3123   Position and secure work surfaces
- L/600/3215   Attach fittings to a finished interior

Source: Register of Regulated Qualifications (England, Wales and Northern Ireland)

Flexibility

It is worth thinking about how flexible you want your qualification to be in terms of the subjects covered. To establish the flexibility of a qualification ask the following questions:

✓ What units do you have to study, and what units are optional?

✓ What is the balance between the number of compulsory units and the number of optional units available to you?

✓ How different are the optional units from the main focus of the qualification?

Case study
Jenny searching for the right MA in Business Management

Jenny is 29 and works as an account manager in the charity sector. Jenny has conducted an initial review of the website of ten universities in her search for an MA in Business Management. She has found that the mandatory content of many of the MA Business Management programmes is quite similar. What has attracted her to one particular MA programme is the range of elective or optional modules she can take. The university allows her to select three optional modules from a wide variety of 12. Furthermore, a number of these modules provide a real scope for specialisation. One in particular is perfect for her needs entitled 'Management in the public sector'.

Learning outcomes

Each unit should have defined learning outcomes which should be available for you to see. *Learning outcomes* are what you are expected to know, understand or do as a consequence of your learning. Learning outcomes are the bread and butter of a good qualification. They map what learning you should have gained as you work through each unit in a qualification and what you will be assessed on at the end of each unit. The nature of the learning outcomes will depend on the level of difficulty of the qualification. Most national qualifications are grouped together at different levels of difficulty. The importance of levels is explained in Chapter 3. A qualification which does not have clearly defined learning outcomes is to be avoided. Without learning outcomes you do not have the necessary information to review your progress properly.

Exhibit 2 An example of learning outcomes

Diploma in Business and Administration

Learners must know and understand:
1. The concept, purpose and sources of money
2. The commonly used sources of financial advice and how such advice can help with making informed financial decisions

Learners must be able to:
1. Manage personal money through budgeting
2. Plan for future expenditure
3. Select a personal current account and a savings account appropriate to their needs

Source: Ofqual, Diploma qualification criteria, 2009

The importance of good titling

The qualification title needs to be clear and accurate. It should give you a sense of the level of difficulty and a strong indication of content. The same is true of the titles of units and modules that make up a qualification. It should be obvious what each unit or module is covering so that you can make a judgement on whether the qualification is coherent. If a qualification is regulated by one of the education authorities in the UK then its titling will need to meet particular requirements on accuracy designed to support you make clear choices as a consumer.

Understanding the content of university qualifications

Obviously higher level qualifications, such as bachelors and masters degrees, might well contain unfamiliar modules because the qualifications contain some highly specialised content. For example in Exhibit 3, describing the unit structure of a bachelor's degree in Italian, a number of the optional modules offered have titles which require a high degree of specialist knowledge to understand. You have the right to know what you are spending your money on so always search for more information or phone the relevant department, using the admissions contact information provided on the website. Don't be afraid to ask the obvious question, 'what does this module cover?'

Exhibit 3 An example of module titles in a BA in Italian

Bachelor's degree in Italian

Compulsory courses
Italian Language 1
Optional courses
You will select 3.0 credits from a wide range of options. Options may include:

Modern Authors II
Realism and Neo-Realism
Problems in Italian History, 1848-1915
History of Twentieth-Century Italian Design
Background to Dante and the Inferno
Introduction to Linguistics and Syntactic Theory
Contemporary Italian Narrative Literature and Cinema
Risorgimento Histories
From World War II to the 21st Century

Source: UCL Website 2011

The length of a qualification

You need clear information on the time commitment involved in taking a qualification. For example you need to know how many hours a week you are required to attend to classes and also a reasonable estimate of the time needed for your own study.

Different systems are used to measure the time commitment involved in taking a qualification. One common system is the use of *guided learning hours* (GLH). GLH measures your supervised learning, which is the time spent learning under the supervision of a teacher or coordinator. However the GLH does not represent the full commitment of your time and does not attempt to measure the study time you will need to commit outside of the classroom or workshop, working on assignments, research or revision. You will need to conduct further research to find this information.

University qualifications use *nominal learning hours* to measure the length of a qualification. In contrast to GLH this measurement includes an approximate value of the private study time required to complete a qualification. Private study includes the preparation for seminars, independent reading, revision and coursework involved in studying a qualification at university.

Credit

Measurements such as guided learning hours and nominal learning hours are used to work out the credit value of a qualification. In a *credit system*, a qualification and each of its units has a credit value. One unit of credit describes a particular period of learning. So the total amount of credit tells you how long the qualification will take to complete. It should be noted that the term credit is used both as a measurement of time and to denote the achievement of a unit.

Exhibit 4 How credit is measured in the Qualifications and Credit Framework

---

The Qualifications and Credit Framework

In the Qualifications and Credit Framework (QCF) in England, Wales and Northern Ireland there are three different sizes of qualification available to take. Qualifications are either classified as Awards, Certificates or Diplomas in this framework. In the QCF, one unit of credit describes 10 hours of guided learning.

- An Award is a qualification of 1-12 credits
- A Certificate is a qualification of between 13-36 credits
- A Diploma is a qualification of 37 credits or more

Source: Ofqual website 2011

Note that the amount of credit attached to a particular qualification varies according to the duration of a qualification but does not vary according to the difficulty of a qualification. *Higher level qualifications* do not gain more credit. Credit is a way of comparing qualifications of the same level.

One unit of credit represents 10 hours of learning in the university system in the UK, using the wider definition of learning which includes private study, referred to as nominal learning hours. A typical university module is 30 credits which represents 300 hours of learning. A bachelor's degree with honours is 360 credits.

Transferring learning with credit

The other important benefit of credit is flexibility. Traditionally, once you started a qualification, you then had to complete all the units within that qualification, often within a set time. If you did not complete all the units in time you did not get the qualification and you wasted a great deal of effort. The credit system helps deal with this problem. You still need to complete particular units. However, if you do a unit and then stop for two years, your units effectively get placed in a bank. You can move forward with those units at a later point, when you are ready to start learning again. Note, however, that there are still time limits.

The credit system also allows flexibility in terms of *where* you use your units. Again, traditionally you were bound by what was available to study within a particular qualification. Under the credit system you can potentially transfer units of learning between different qualifications. This means that you can start one qualification and change your mind half way through but still potentially use the units you have gained towards another qualification.

Credit transfer schemes commonly allow you to use the credit gained in one qualification towards another, higher level qualification. Note, however, that the admissions procedures of a particular college or university will determine which qualifications qualify as *prior learning*. Different terms are used in the qualifications world to describe this process including the *recognition of prior achievement* and the *accreditation of prior learning*.

> **Case study**
> *Veronica moving to a new address*
>
> Veronica wants to do a part-time qualification in counselling. There is a possibility that Veronica will be moving to a different part of the country and she wants the option to 'park' her qualification and continue her learning at a different college when she is ready.

Veronica also wants to retain some flexibility as to which area of counselling she specialises in.

Veronica speaks to her local college. They say that if she takes a qualification in the Qualification and Credit Framework (QCF), she can then 'bank' the units she gains until she is ready to restart, subject to certain time limits. Veronica will then ask colleges in her new locality what qualifications they offer to build on the units she has already gained.

> **Case study**
> *John establishing whether his learning will count to a qualification*

John is 19 and lives in Glasgow. John has just completed his Higher National Certificate (HNC) in Agriculture at a local college and has gained 120 credit points. John has a strong interest in agricultural management and has found a number of suitable degree programmes in this area. He is concerned that he might have to repeat significant amounts of learning he gained in his HNC. The admissions officers of the universities he is interested in confirm that the credit he has gained will count towards his degree programme and gives him an *exemption* from modules in the first year of study.

Recognising other types of learning

Another important aspect of the growth of a credit-based system is that different types of learning are now being captured as units with credit. In the past, training in the private sector often did not lead to a qualification. Increasingly, units and qualifications with credit are being developed by employers such as McDonalds, Flybe and Network Rail. This trend is very positive as it means that work-based training not only develops you, but now can count towards a nationally recognised qualification.

You should also be aware that *informal learning* – that is learning gained in the workplace that sits outside of a unit or qualification and therefore is not formally recognised – might still be able to contribute to a qualification you are considering.

Case study
David establishing whether his learning will count to a qualification

David has worked in the hospitality industry for over seven years and during that time he has developed a significant body of knowledge and skills in this area. He has also attended a variety of training programmes. He is considering taking a qualification in hospitality as the next step in his career. David should contact the learning provider he is interested in and establish whether they recognise informal learning as contributing to their qualifications. If they do, David should spend time summarising the knowledge and skills he has gained and mapping this to the qualification. He can then present this evidence to the admissions tutor. It is possible that the learning provider will recognise this prior learning and accredit the learning as part of the qualification.

Future developments
The use of credit is well-established in Scotland and across higher education in the UK. The use of credit in vocational qualifications in England, Wales and Northern Ireland is still in its infancy. The majority of high profile national qualifications in these countries still do not use a credit system. There have been teething problems for some of the new credit-based qualifications that have been recently introduced. Despite this, credit systems are gradually becoming established and are likely to become standard in countries within the European Union and elsewhere. This is good for you as a learner. It makes taking a qualification more flexible, reduces the likelihood of wasting effort on unused units, and gives you more consumer choice because of the greater range of units you can potentially incorporate into a qualification.

Assessment

All qualifications are assessed in some way. This means that you have to demonstrate what you have learnt to someone else. You are usually assessed at the end of each unit in a qualification. The type of assessment might vary between units. To pass a qualification you might need to pass the assessments in all units or just some of them. The threshold for success or failure varies between different kinds of qualifications.

You are assessed against the learning outcomes in each unit. We emphasised that a good qualification will have clear learning outcomes for each unit. It should be obvious what you need to learn in that unit and the information should be presented in a way which is both easy to find and understand. You should also be given a clear explanation as to how each unit will be assessed; this is often called the *assessment criteria*. This information should be available in the brochure or on the internet site which describes the qualification.

You may be assessed by answering exam questions in a *supervised environment*, within a set period of time. There are often rules you need to obey in this type of environment: for example, not talking, having your mobile phone switched off, and not bringing course material into the exam room. These rules are typically enforced by an *invigilator* who supervises the exam hall. For some types of qualification your answer sheets are then sent to an *external examiner,* who will not be known to you. An examiner is a person whose job it is to mark your work. An examiner is usually an expert in the subject you are studying and in this type of assessment is not your teacher. This form of assessment is often called *external assessment*.

You might well sit end of year exams at university with one important difference from the model described above. Your exams will be marked by your course tutors. Their marking will be quality assured by an examination panel which will typically contain an independent examiner not involved in the teaching of your course.

Alternatively your work might be *continuously assessed* by your teacher in teaching sessions. The teacher, acting as your *assessor*, will be constantly looking for evidence of the necessary skills against the assessment criteria. Instead of a high-pressured exam in supervised conditions, the focus is now on a long-term process of discussion and review. This type of assessment is often called *internal assessment*.

However you are assessed, you might well come across the term *authentication*. In the context of qualifications this means being able to identify you correctly as the person who has produced a particular piece of work for assessment and it also ensures that your work is original and not copied from some other source.

The terms *assessor* and *examiner* both refer to the person who assesses your work. An examiner is often used to describe the person in the first scenario described above and the term assessor is more commonly used in the second scenario. These different types of assessment make different demands on you, but also different demands on the people assessing your work.

Some assessment requires the people assessing your work to make subjective judgements. They need to judge whether you have met the standard needed to pass the qualification. This would be the case in a doctorate, where your assessor, having read your thesis and interviewed you, would make a judgement on whether to award you a PhD. Other assessments require the people assessing you to perform more of a mechanical function. In a multiple choice assessment, for example, the assessor is simply checking whether you have the right or wrong answer. Increasingly this is conducted automatically, by computer.

Assessments can be marked in different ways. Some national qualifications in the UK use a *pass*, *fail*, *merit* and *distinction*, while others are graded alphabetically from an A* or A grade, down to a G, with U which is ungraded. This type of grading system requires a more complex system of scoring to establish the boundaries between the different *grades*.

You can be assessed at different stages in a qualification. You might be assessed at the start of the qualification to establish your strengths and weaknesses as a learner. This is called *diagnostic assessment*. Your progress might be assessed as you work through the unit or module of a qualification. This is important as it allows you to reflect on your own learning and prepare for exams. This type of assessment is called *formative assessment*. Your formal assessment against the learning outcomes of a unit is called *summative assessment*.

Special requirements
All nationally recognised qualifications have a legal duty not to discriminate against someone with any form of special need or disability. This means they have to make *reasonable adjustments*, which enable you to participate fully in a qualification and to be assessed in a way that takes into consideration your particular requirements. So, if you are dyslexic

you probably qualify for extra time when sitting a written exam. If you are sight-impaired you have a right to test papers formatted in large print or Braille. If you are hearing-impaired you might have the right to do an exam using sign language.

It is up to the organisation responsible for the qualification to ensure that these reasonable adjustments are in place. What this organisation cannot do is give you an unfair advantage over other learners and they need to balance making reasonable adjustments with maintaining the standard of the qualification. Certain disabilities inevitably prevent you meeting the standards of certain qualifications – if you are visually impaired you won't be able to train as an airline pilot. However, with these exceptions, the emphasis should always be on how you can be supported in undertaking a qualification in a way that helps you manage any special requirements.

You also have a right to expect organisations conducting assessments to make *special considerations* in the event of unforeseen circumstances which affect your performance on the day of an exam. For example, if you suffer the death of a close relative in the period around an examination, the organisation responsible for your assessment has an obligation to take this into consideration and either make alternative arrangements or reflect your circumstances in the mark they give you.

How do you like to learn?

As a qualification consumer you need to consider which type of qualification will best suit your learning style. This requires an awareness of your own strengths and weaknesses. These are some of the questions you need to ask yourself:

- ✓ Do you prefer learning in an applied way with an emphasis on developing practical skills? Or would you prefer learning in a theoretical way with an emphasis on exploring theories and concepts?

- ✓ Are you best suited to studying hard for a final exam, or do you prefer producing written work which is continuously assessed over time?

✓ Do you want to learn gradually, over a long period of time or would you prefer a short, intense course?

✓ Do you prefer learning in a social environment in lectures, seminar groups and workshops, or do you prefer to learn by yourself or with a *private tutor*?

✓ Do you want to learn while you work and be able to practise and apply your skills in the workplace?

✓ Do you want to learn in a structured environment or flexibly in your own time?

Some of the answers to these questions will be defined by the nature of the qualification you are interested in. However, it is always worth conducting an initial review to establish whether a qualification suits your own learning style.

Some vocabulary

A *course* roughly describes structured learning over a period of time, characterised by some form of attendance and assessment. Many courses do not lead to recognised qualifications. While a course which does not lead to a qualification might be appropriate for your needs, if you are in doubt about the status of a course always phone up and check before spending any money.

The term *award* is used interchangeably with *qualification* and *certificate*, but is also used to describe the end point when you successfully gain the qualification. It is common to hear the phrase 'you have been awarded the qualification' which means you have completed the requirements of the qualification and have been given the certificate.

A *qualification* typically requires some form of assessment, but there are exceptions. Some professional bodies and trade associations award qualifications that are recognised in a profession but not obtained by an examination. These qualifications are often awarded on the basis of experience and typically lead to membership in that professional body or trade association.

Training encompasses learning that happens both inside and outside of a qualification. A great deal of the training you receive in your lifetime occurs in the workplace and is different from the training involved in gaining a particular qualification. The word *training* often refers to the development of the skills needed for a particular job. Phrases such as 'on-the-job training' or being 'trained-up' are commonly used in the workplace. In recent years there has been a concerted drive by the education authorities to capture the wide variety of skills you gain through on-the-job training within an officially recognised qualification.

Another important distinction is between formal, informal and non-formal learning. *Formal learning* describes the structured learning you undertake towards a qualification or course. This type of learning is supervised in some way. *Informal learning* is the intentional learning you do in a particular subject, which is done in your own time for your own benefit. *Non-formal learning* is the learning you do naturally at work or in other environments.

Chapter 2
The qualification system in the UK

This chapter:

- → Explains how qualifications are developed in the UK

- → Describes the important differences between the organisation which develops the qualification and the organisation which teaches you the qualification

- → Outlines how qualifications are quality assured

- → Provides examples of the different ways qualifications are delivered to you

Why the qualification system in the UK can be so confusing

Just as there are differences between Dell, Hewlett Packard and Apple computers, there is also a difference between the companies that develop qualifications in the UK, and thus the quality of the different qualification products. The fact that these organisations are often not responsible for teaching the qualification does not mean they are irrelevant to the learning experience. In the UK there are many organisations which develop but do not teach qualifications. While you may not have much day-to-day contact with these organisations they are often ultimately accountable for your qualification. Their role is very important to you as a consumer and will be explained in more detail later in this chapter.

> **Case study**
> *Ben searching for the right graphic design qualification*
>
> Ben is confused by the information he is reading while searching for graphic design qualifications. There are business names against the different qualifications that he is not familiar with. Moreover these organisations are not the colleges he is considering studying at. For example he sees three very similar graphic design qualifications but one states 'Edexcel' in its title, one states 'OCR' and one 'City and Guilds'. Does it matter which of these three qualifications he selects?
>
> The answer is yes! Imagine if Ben was buying a new computer. He would have two decisions to make. Firstly, which supplier will he buy the computer from? He might go to one of several high street stores or he might go online. Secondly, which make of computer will he buy? 10 different manufacturers might have their computers available through these outlets.

Some organisations both develop and teach their own qualifications. Universities and chartered institutes are examples of organisations which perform both roles. In some ways this makes life more straightforward for you as a consumer. If you have a problem with the quality of teaching, the quality of resources or the quality of marking, it is the university or institute you speak to as the accountable organisation.

The free market in qualifications

The qualifications market for both adults and young people in the UK is essentially a free market. This means private companies compete to offer qualifications either directly to you or to schools, colleges and other organisations who will then offer you the qualification. What is distinctive about the UK market for qualifications is that this competition not only exists in the market for adult qualifications but also in the market for school qualifications. A typical secondary school in England can choose the qualifications it buys from a number of competing companies. These companies compete on the content, structure and assessment of their qualifications, the support and resources they provide the school, and also on price.

This is different from how qualifications are offered in many other countries. For example, an 18-year-old learner in France typically takes the French Baccalaureate in their final year of lycée. This qualification is owned and delivered by the state. There is not the same choice as for a school or a learner in the UK. Equally, there are not the issues faced in the UK's free market system, about regulation and whether the qualification standard is secure between competing providers.

While the UK has a free market for qualifications, government and education authorities have a major role to play both in ensuring the quality of the qualifications you take and also helping you meet the cost of those qualifications. For many qualifications, government funding means that you do not need to pay, or only have to pay a limited amount. In the UK, for example, the *local authorities* will pay the main fees for any young person under the age of 19 to take a qualification in full-time education.

Qualification developers

The organisations that design the qualifications you take are called *qualification developers*. A qualification developer decides the content and level of the qualification and how it will be assessed. Some organisations, such as universities, also teach the qualifications they develop. Most sell their qualifications to schools, colleges and other learning providers who then teach them. The government and education authorities also play an important role in defining the rules and guidelines governing the development of many national qualifications.

The qualifications market in the UK is very large. Hundreds of different organisations of all shapes and sizes develop qualifications. Some qualifications are taken by hundreds of thousands of learners each year, such as GCSEs or Scottish Highers. Other qualifications can be described as 'niche'. These qualifications, in specialist areas such as horseshoe making or spectacle making, are developed by a small number of organisations for a small number of people. Four of the main types of organisation involved in the development of qualifications are outlined below.

Awarding organisations
You might well come across the term *awarding organisation*, *awarding body* or *exam board*. These words are used interchangeably. Awarding organisations develop and sell qualifications to schools, colleges and other learning providers but do not deliver (teach) those qualifications.

Awarding organisations are responsible for ensuring the assessment used in a qualification is fair. This means your work will be marked in a consistent and accurate way. If a college buys a qualification from an awarding organisation they will need to teach the content stipulated by the awarding organisation. The college has to assess you in adherence to the rules set out by the awarding organisation. It is typically the awarding organisation that awards you the qualification and issues you with a certificate.

Universities
Universities are also responsible for developing, delivering and checking the quality of their own qualifications. Universities can be compared to the supermarket chains that produce a range of their own-brand products. Universities are overseen by the education authorities in the UK and are largely financed through the Higher Education Funding Councils. However as institutions they have a strong degree of autonomy. It is up to the management of a particular university as to what degrees and other qualifications they will offer, and which learners they will accept to study their qualifications.

Higher education qualifications such as bachelors and masters degrees are usually developed, delivered and awarded by the same organisation. These organisations are described as having full *degree awarding powers*. *Listed colleges* are an exception. A listed college is an organisation recognised by a university and by the UK government as having sufficient expertise to develop and deliver the modules of a higher education qualification. The qualification is then awarded by the partner university.

Professional organisations
The term *professional organisation* is used here to describe organisations such as chartered institutes, royal institutes and other bodies which are responsible for developing people in a particular profession. There are numerous professional organisations in areas as diverse as marketing, insurance, architecture and ship building. These organisations are often responsible for developing and teaching the qualification or suite of qualifications that form the entry requirements to gain qualified status in that profession.

Employers
Employers may develop and teach their own qualifications. More and more large companies are turning training programmes into nationally-recognised qualifications. They are doing this by gaining official recognition and positioning their qualifications at particular levels in the UK national qualifications frameworks. Their qualifications are then quality assured by the relevant education authorities.

> **Example**
> *McDonalds and its nationally-recognised qualifications*
>
> McDonalds has always had a strong reputation for developing its staff. Its five star training system is widely viewed as an example of good practice in ensuring staff feel a sense of motivation and progression. McDonalds wanted to take this one step further and gain formal recognition for their training programmes from the UK education authorities. McDonalds now offers a basic shift manager's course which is nationally recognised at level 1 and 2 in the Qualifications and Credit Framework (QCF) in England, Wales and Northern Ireland. The fact that McDonalds qualifications now sit on national

framework levels gives these qualifications greater status. Employees can take pride in the fact that their qualifications are equivalent in standard to other major national qualifications such as NVQs and GCSEs.

Quality assurance

Quality assurance is particularly important in the arena of qualifications. Quality assurance describes the process of checking the quality of qualifications and units against a defined standard. It is vital to keep on checking that learners across the different parts of the country are having the same high quality experience when undertaking a qualification. Quality assurance is often undertaken by an external body that is independent from the organisations which develop, teach and assess the qualification.

All high profile national qualifications are subject to some form of quality assurance by the education authorities in the UK. In Chapter 1 we defined the term *education authorities* broadly to describe the agencies, regulators and inspectorates who are responsible for safeguarding the quality of qualifications and teaching.

Quality assurance occurs at different stages in the life of a qualification:

- Many qualification developers are scrutinised at the organisational level by the education authorities to make sure they have the resources and expertise to develop high quality qualifications.

- Individual qualifications, and the units within them, are reviewed in the early stages of their development and also when they are formally submitted into national qualification frameworks.

- Learning providers are regularly monitored by inspectors reviewing the teaching across different locations.

- The assessment of a qualification is quality assured on an ongoing basis by the qualification developer, by moderating samples of real assessments and by checking that the marking is consistent and accurate.

Case study
How the quality of a qualification is checked

A qualification developer wants to develop a new Health and Safety qualification at level 2 in one of the national qualification frameworks in the UK. As a first step, the organisation applies to be recognised by the education authorities. This process involves demonstrating the necessary expertise to design and assess health and safety qualifications. The education authorities also scrutinize areas such as customer service and the management and security of data against quality standards. The organisation then develops its qualification. For this to be offered at level 2, its content might well be reviewed by both health and safety experts and also by qualification experts to ensure that the qualification is at the right level of difficulty for a level 2 submission.

The qualification developer then sells the new qualification to a number of colleges across the region. It conducts quality checks to ensure a college has the teaching expertise and resources to effectively deliver the qualification and runs a series of training sessions to train teachers on the assessment requirements in Health and Safety. The college then teaches and assesses the qualification, working to the rules of the qualification developer. After the first series of assessments the qualification developer conducts sample checks to make sure learners are being assessed fairly. In the second year of the qualification, a government inspectorate reviews the quality of teaching in Health and Safety as part of its wider review of the college.

The way quality is checked is different in universities and other higher education institutions. The Quality Assurance Agency conducts quality reviews which highlight good practice and make recommendations for improvements and these reports are made publicly available. However, unlike schools and colleges, universities manage their own internal quality assurance. This means they are responsible for the standard of qualifications and teaching they provide. Universities also employ independent reviewers to help ensure quality. In the marking of assignments in an MA programme, for example, a university will ensure that their examination panel includes an independent examiner to scrutinise the standard of marking.

The role of Sector Skills Councils
Sector Skills Councils (SSCs) are responsible for representing the voice of employers in relation to the development of skills in a particular sector or industry. They represent roughly 90% of the workforce. Each Sector Skills Council works with employers to identify which skills need addressing through the development of qualifications in their sector. Each Sector Skills Council is the owner of a *national occupational standard (NOS)*. A national occupational standard outlines the knowledge, skills and understanding you need to gain entry into a particular profession, such as IT or engineering. It is also the blueprint for what qualifications should contain in that sector.

It is the responsibility of the SSC to ensure that this blueprint remains current. Any organisation which wants to develop nationally-recognised qualifications in a particular sector in the UK needs to talk to the appropriate SSC and needs to make sure they cover the national occupational standards for that sector.

The qualification system is subject to change in the UK. To find a list of the current SSCs contact the Alliance of Sector Skills Councils. This body acts as a single voice for SSCs and retains an up-to-date list of the current SSCs in the UK.

The delivery of qualifications

Once a qualification has been developed it is then ready to be taught or delivered. The most important organisation for you is likely to be the learning provider that teaches you. For simplicity in this book we use the word *learning provider* to describe the different types of organisation delivering qualifications. Your relationship with your teacher or supervisor is one of the most important aspects of your learning experience. They will be your first point of contact for day-to-day issues and questions. Other staff might also play an important role in your learning experience, such as the receptionist, welfare officer, librarian, social programme coordinator and examinations officer. The examinations officer, for example, conducts a number of important transactions on your behalf. They will typically manage your entry onto the qualification, record the results you achieve and send these results to the organisation which is responsible for the qualification, if that is a different organisation.

The learning provider will often represent your interests, even by dealing with issues outside of their direct control. For example in many cases a question about your results has to be raised with the qualification developer. However, your learning provider will probably contact the qualification developer and manage the enquiry process for you. Many learners will have little or no contact with the qualification developer and might not even be fully aware of who they are.

While there are variations across the UK, one can divide the UK education system into distinct stages and sectors defined in part by age. Primary education caters for young children up to the age of 11. Secondary education caters for young people between 11 and 16 and ends with compulsory examinations, such as GCSEs and Scottish Qualification Certificates. Since 1992, young people up to the age of 16 have followed the national curriculum, which outlines a broad framework of subjects. The national curriculum is compulsory in publicly funded schools, often referred to as *state* or *maintained* schools. It should also be noted there is a strong private sector in both primary and secondary education which offers qualifications both within and outside of the national curriculum.

Education up until the age of 19 is publicly funded through local education authorities in England and Wales, through education authorities in Scotland and through five Education and Library Boards in Northern Ireland. A growing number of state schools are applying for *academy status* that gives the school control over their own budget.

The Education Act of 2008 made education compulsory until the age of 18, although this does not come into full effect until 2015. At 16 young people have a range of options including taking *general qualifications* which are designed for entry into university or a wide variety of *vocational qualifications* focused on developing and applying the skills needed for the workplace. Young people typically take their final examinations for qualifications such as A levels, the Welsh Baccalaureate and Scottish Highers at the age of 17 or 18. Some young people, particularly in private schools, may take the International Baccalaureate and Cambridge Pre U at this age.

Many schools provide sixth forms for 16-18 year olds, but further education (FE) colleges and a range of other learning providers also offer examinations for this age group. In terms of funding, young people are fully funded up until the age of 19. Many of the qualifications offered to the 16-19 age group are also offered to adults and this sector is often described as *further education*.

The education system in the UK is subject to frequent changes, as new governments look to address perceived failings. The type of qualifications offered to young people between the ages of 14-19 is a particularly controversial issue. A report by Alison Wolf (the Wolf Report, *Review of Vocational Education,* March 2011), criticised the tendency of many schools to offer 'low quality' vocational qualifications to their less able students. She argued that this was partly motivated by the desire to increase performance points achieved by a school. Her recommendations centred on the need to ensure learners did not leave school without achieving qualification in the core skills of maths and English. She also advocated that schools, working with colleges, should focus on a smaller number of high quality vocational qualifications such as apprenticeships.

Higher education typically refers to bachelors degrees, masters degrees and other postgraduate qualifications provided by universities and other *higher education institutions*.

Adult education or *lifelong learning* describes the diverse range of qualifications available for adults at any age. A wide range of learning providers including FE colleges, employers, private colleges, internet learning providers and prisons offer qualifications to adult learners. There is also great flexibility in how you can learn, from taking an evening course at your college to learning in your own time over the internet. Because of this diversity we often use the term *qualification delivery* rather than teaching to highlight the variety of ways you can study a qualification and the variety of different places in which learning can take place.

Annex 2 at the end of this book defines the different types of organisation that deliver qualifications in the UK.

The case studies below describe a few of the different learning providers in the UK.

Case study
Raj learning Italian

> Raj is 26 and is keen to learn Italian. He wants to study in a social environment where he can meet new people but he also wants to gain a qualification. He visits the CityLit website, the largest adult learning centre in London, and finds an affordable part-time level 1 Italian qualification. He attends one two-hour evening class each week at their central London College which is conveniently on his route back from work.

Case study
John learning numeracy skills

> John is 41 and is serving a six-month prison sentence. John's prison sentence has made him think long and hard about his life and how he can improve it. He decides to enrol on an adult numeracy qualification, which involves four afternoon lessons a week at the prison's learning centre.

Case study
Nancy developing her translation skills

> Nancy is 28 and a working mum. Nancy is starting up her own online translation business and wants to further develop her language skills by studying a Level 7 Diploma in Translation. She wants to study flexibly at home and in her own time to gain the skills and qualifications to move forward in her career. Nancy finds a qualification which is primarily based on independent study through an internet-based learning company. Nancy is assigned an online tutor who she communicates with by email and through Skype. She periodically emails her assignments and gets feedback emailed back to her.

Case study
Jesmond taking an MA in Technology Management

Jesmond wants to do an MA in Technology Management. He wants to learn primarily from home, but to have some contact time with his course tutors and fellow students. He wants the option of taking breaks between modules, and the confidence that if he does not complete the full MA he can still gain a qualification. Jesmond visits the Open University (OU) website and finds a suitable qualification. He reads the 'study explained' section of the website and also phones a learning adviser to clarify how his distance learning would be managed. He establishes he will have the security of being able to claim a Postgraduate Certificate and Diploma if he only completes a certain number of modules. It is also confirmed to him that he can study primarily from home, but will be in frequent contact with his tutor and will have the option of attending a number of seminars with fellow students. Jesmond decides to register on the qualification. Distance learning can be defined as home-based study involving learning through the internet, phone and correspondence.

Case study
Clement developing skills in office administration

Clement is 42 years old and studying for his Level 2 NVQ in Office Administration. Clement's workplace is his learning environment. Through doing his normal job and recording the techniques and methods he adopts to complete daily tasks, he is fulfilling the competencies required by the qualification. He is compiling a portfolio of evidence which is then being assessed by an external assessor from the awarding organisation. An external assessor is an individual who has been trained to review and assess work for a particular qualification. Clement is being supported by his employer in studying for his qualification and he is in direct contact with the awarding organisation for all his needs.

Chapter 3
How to choose the right level of qualification

This chapter:

→ Describes how to establish the level of a qualification

→ Explains how to use the information in a qualification framework to decide on the right qualification

→ Explains how to use the UCAS Tariff Points system

→ Outlines the questions you should ask about the level of a qualification

The significance of 'level'

In the world of qualifications the word *level* has quite a precise meaning. To help group and describe qualifications the education authorities have developed *qualifications frameworks* which are maps of the qualifications in the system. Qualification frameworks are organised in terms of levels. The levels start at entry level or level 1 and go up from there. The higher the level, the more difficult the qualification.

Frameworks give you important information on which qualification to select to gain entry into a particular job. They allow teachers to decide the appropriate qualification to teach, and employers and admission tutors to set entry requirements and to compare the value of different qualifications. A qualification framework is a type of map. You can use this map to work out which qualification or qualifications you need to get to a destination and how long the journey will take to get there.

Qualification frameworks support *progression* towards a particular goal through your learning. Progression does not necessarily mean taking just one qualification. Progression towards a career goal might involve taking several qualifications over a period of years. A qualification framework which groups qualifications at different levels allows you to plan your progression.

A qualification level does not define how long a qualification takes, or what age you need to be to take that qualification. Some qualifications lasting for one month sit at the same level as qualifications lasting for three years. A qualification at a higher level will not necessarily have a longer exam, require you to memorise more information, or require you to work harder. What counts is the skills you will have demonstrated in successfully gaining that qualification. A higher level qualification develops higher level skills. These differences underpin the different qualification levels in the UK.

One of the main drivers of the level of different qualifications is how independently they require you to work. In a level 1 qualification a lot of your learning is supported by someone else. In a level 6 qualification a lot of your learning is independent. As the qualification levels become progressively more difficult you are expected to demonstrate increasingly higher level skills. Qualifications at low national levels often involve following instructions to complete simple tasks or solve simple problems. Qualifications at the higher national levels typically require you to demonstrate a range of higher level skills such as identifying and solving complex problems, critically reviewing content, conducting detailed investigations into a particular subject, developing new approaches to a particular task, adapting to changing requirements and effectively planning, organising and evaluating your own learning.

Some examples of the different skills developed at different qualification levels are highlighted below. These examples are taken from one of the major national qualification frameworks in the UK.

Exhibit 5 Examples of skills required at different qualification levels

A qualification at entry level Qualifications at this level include qualifications developing foundation skills in literacy, numeracy and IT.
- Carry out simple, familiar tasks and activities.
- Follow instructions to use rehearsed steps to complete tasks and activities.
- With appropriate guidance begin to take responsiblity for the outcomes of simple tasks.

A qualification at level 3 Qualifications at this level include qualifications giving you entry to university.
- Have awareness of different perspectives or approaches within the area of study of work.
- Address problems that, while well defined, may be complex and non routine.
- Use appropriate investigation to inform actions.
- Take responsibility for initiating and completing tasks and procedures, including where relevant, responsiblity for supervising or guiding others.

A qualification at level 6 Qualifications at this level include university degrees and high level vocational qualifications.
- Evaluate actions, methods and results and their implications.
- Determine, refine, adapt and use appropriate methods and skills.
- Initiate and lead tasks and processes, taking responsibility where relevant, for the work and roles of others.
- Exercise broad autonomy and judgement.

Source: Ofqual website, QCF, 2011

A higher level qualification is not necessarily a better qualification. The quality of teaching, the quality of assessment and the quality of resources do not change between qualification levels. All of the qualifications sitting in one of the national frameworks, at whatever level, need to meet the same quality requirements.

Getting the right information from a complex system

In an ideal world there would be one major qualification framework containing all the major qualifications. Instead there are a number of different qualification frameworks in the UK. This can be partially explained by the separate powers enjoyed by Scotland and Wales in managing their own qualifications system. There are times when the differences between frameworks will matter to you. For example, if you are moving from England to Scotland and want to know whether your qualification will be recognised. Chapter 9 explains what to do in this situation. In general, you will not often have to compare the levels of different frameworks.

If you are shopping for a nationally recognised qualification, what is important is to know in which framework your qualification can be found, as a means of checking whether the level is right for you. You want to use your money wisely so it is important to understand the significance of the level of the qualification and how it maps to other levels in that qualification framework. The questions at the end of this chapter help you to make effective judgements on the right level of a qualification.

The UCAS Tariff system

The *University and College Admissions Service (UCAS) Tariff* is a point system used by universities to compare the different qualifications that allow you to gain entry onto an undergraduate course in higher education. Only certain qualifications are allocated UCAS Tariff and accepted by UK universities as evidence of the skills needed to enter university. If a qualification does not have UCAS Tariff this does not make it a poor qualification. Many excellent qualifications designed for the workplace are not given UCAS Tariff and employers should not use UCAS Tariff as a means of judging the quality of a qualification.

How does it work?

The UCAS organisation works with universities and qualification developers to allocate a particular number of tariff points to qualifications they believe are suitable for entry into university. The amount of tariff given to a qualification is based on a judgement as to how demanding and how time consuming the qualification is for the learner. The level of UCAS Tariff you gain for a qualification varies depending on the mark you gain in that qualification. For example, a grade A in a Scottish Higher will attract more tariff points than a grade C. Most UK universities use this system to make conditional offers to students applying for courses. A conditional offer is an offer of a university place dependent on the students achieving the required tariff points and grades.

When considering which qualification to take it is worth asking the following questions to establish the difficulty of a qualification:

- ✓ What information does the qualification title give you about its level of difficulty? A good title will highlight its level in some form. However, be careful, there are lots of overused titling conventions such as 'Diploma' and 'Certificate' which are used for qualifications at many different levels. Always be prepared to interrogate further.

- ✓ Is your qualification recognised at a particular level in a national qualifications framework in the UK? You should always be able to find this out on the page of information explaining the qualification to you.

- ✓ If you are hoping to get a job or gain entry into further or higher education establish which qualifications meet these entry requirements. This information should be clearly set out in a job advert or page of course details relating to a particular qualification. If not, phone up and find out. There are national agencies that can help you with this. How to get this help is explained in Chapter 8.

- ✓ Interrogate what skills are being developed by a qualification at a particular level. This information should be available in the page of course details on the website or in the brochure of the learning provider. You need to get a feel for whether the qualification is about right, too difficult or too easy for your purpose.

- ✓ All national qualification frameworks use *level indicators* and level descriptors. These are statements describing the skills developed at a particular qualification level. This will help establish whether the qualification is at the right level for your needs though these level indicators and level descriptors are very generic.

- ✓ For more information about the national qualification frameworks in the UK go to Annex 1, which sets out each framework. Some of the major qualifications available at the different qualification levels are also highlighted for your reference.

Chapter 4
How to judge the cost of a qualification

This chapter:

- → Explains what makes up the cost of a qualification

- → Clarifies what you should look for in terms of cost information

- → Highlights the difficulty in comparing the costs of qualifications in the UK

- → Explains the importance of establishing what funding is available and where to go for more information

- → Provides you with examples of the different types of funding available

One of the most important considerations in selecting a qualification is determining whether it is affordable. Unfortunately it can be hard to determine whether the cost of a qualification is reasonable. It can be hard to find out what a qualification actually costs. Some organisations disclose this information on their websites, for others you have to phone or get hold of a brochure to access this information. There may be several components to the cost; for example, tuition fees and examination fees. There is no easy way of quickly comparing the cost of different qualifications. Unlike other products there are no price comparison websites for the qualification industry.

The cost of a qualification

If you do need to pay for your qualification, or at least part of your qualification, then it is important to be clear what your money is being spent on.

Case study
Parveen and her investigation into the cost of a qualification

Parveen is really keen to improve her French. She is on a tight budget and always wants to get value for money. She wants to study part time, two evenings a week. She has found about 10 qualifications, at level 2, in French which are appropriate for her needs. She is now comparing the cost of qualifications offered by both different colleges and by a number of online providers. This is taking time and she has come across some unfamiliar terms. For example, she is not sure she understands the difference between registration fees, tuition fees and examination fees. She also does not understand why a number of qualifications highlight their tuition fees as 'indicative' or 'subject to change'.

Are you paying for each unit or for the whole qualification?

There are typically two ways you can be charged for a qualification. You can be charged upfront for the whole qualification when you register. This may be presented as a cheaper option but be sure to consider the possible consequences. It might be hard to get a refund or partial refund if you do not complete the qualification. Other organisations may require you to register for each unit or module and only charge you on a 'unit by unit' basis as you progress through your qualification.

Could your qualification be free or subject to a concession?

Many qualifications are free to home students. The term *home student* is often used by organisations selling qualifications. This term usually means born in the UK. However, it sometimes applies specifically to being born in one of Scotland, England, Wales or Northern Ireland. For example, if you are born in Scotland you will be exempt from paying tuition fees for Scottish universities, but this exemption does not currently apply if you were born in England.

What are tuition fees/course fees?

The terms *tuition fees* and *course fees* are interchangeable and describe the main fees you pay when you take a qualification. The tuition fee covers the money spent on the teaching, resources and facilities by the organisation delivering the qualification. How much you pay for tuition depends on many things including the subject, the duration of the course, the type of qualification you are taking and your own circumstances. The government also has a role to play in determining the level of tuition fees, for example in the case of university qualifications.

Often learning providers, such as colleges or universities, are unable to specify exactly how much the tuition fee will be for a qualification starting the following academic year. Tuition fees can often be accompanied with the phrases 'indicative' or 'subject to change'. There are a number of reasons for this lack of clarity. It can be hard to predict what the government might do in raising or lowering the thresholds for tuition fees for certain qualifications. There can also be information lags between qualification developers and learning providers. If your local college is uncertain as to how much it will be charged next year by its qualification developer, this will have a knock-on effect of the college being unable to predict accurately what price you will be charged.

In these circumstances the best option is to phone up the learning provider and clarify exactly when prices for your qualification will be confirmed. This situation, where you commit to a course without knowing what it will cost in subsequent years, is a highly frustrating situation for you as a consumer. It is hard to think of a similar situation in other areas of your life, where you might be spending similar amounts of money.

> **Current debates**
> *Tuition fees in higher education*

There has been controversy around the UK government's plan to raise university tuition fees and the potential disincentive this might create for poorer students to attend university. The debate focuses on the need to double and potentially triple the tuition fees paid by students in English universities to meet the funding crisis faced by universities.

It should be noted that a report produced by Lord Browne, 'Securing a sustainable future for higher education: an independent review of higher education funding and student finance' *October 2010,* went even further in suggesting that there should be no upper limit on the tuition fees charged by universities. However the new charges, while subject to an upper limit, still represented a radical change. As higher charges are introduced in 2012/2013 the income threshold for when students have to pay their tuition fees back will also be increased.

Are you an EU or an international student?
There can be a huge difference between what you pay to study a UK qualification if you are a citizen of the European Union (EU) and what you pay as an international student, a citizen from outside the EU. This difference can amount to many thousands of pounds for a single qualification, so make sure you look at the price information appropriate to your status.

It should be noted that the broader category of the European Economic Area (EEA) is used by some UK learning providers to determine fee levels. Either way, as an international student you need to establish your credentials against the current points-based visa system managed by the UK Borders Agency and identify the feasibility and cost involved in applying for a visa.

Registration fees

Some learning providers will charge you a fee to register for a qualification, in addition to the tuition fee. The *registration fee* is an administrative fee covering the costs of your registration with a particular learning provider to study a qualification. It is important to know the difference between the registration fee and the tuition fee as the registration fee is often not refundable, whereas you might be able to get a refund or partial refund on your tuition fees in the event of withdrawal.

Examination fees

You will typically be charged for sitting the examination at the end of each unit or module. Again this may be a separate fee to the tuition fees. The amount you pay in *examination fees* will depend on the type of assessment used. Certain types of assessment are more expensive than others. Formal exams which pay invigilators to ensure the exam rules are being met can cost significant amounts of money. The learning provider then often has the additional cost of sending your work to external examiners to mark. These costs will be passed on to you in some form.

Replacement fees

Another potential fee to check is whether you will be charged if you lose your qualification certificate and need a replacement sent to you. Some organisations simply refuse to reproduce a certificate and will only provide you with a certifying statement of results. They are likely to charge you a lot of money for this service. While this may be an unlikely cost, it is still worth noting.

Refunds

It is very important to establish what the costs will be if you decide to withdraw from your qualification. Again different organisations will have different approaches and you need to be careful. It is likely to depend greatly on whether you withdraw before the start of the qualification. You need to read the rules in relation to refunds so that you are clear on what to expect.

Other important costs to consider before taking a qualification

There are lots of other costs that you need to think about in budgeting for a qualification. A major cost can be the course books and materials you will need and usually these are not included in the tuition or course fee. To keep costs down you can always look for second-hand versions of the course books, cheaper retailers or even put an advertisement up in your place of learning to see whether any previous students would be willing to sell you their course books. You might be required to join a library or professional body. You might be required to pay a lump sum to gain access to the computer centre of the learning provider. Finally there are costs such as stationery and computer equipment that can quickly add up.

The benefits of belonging to the National Union of Students

It is always worth checking if a qualification you are interested in makes you eligible for membership of the National Union of Students (NUS) and in particular, the NUS Extra Card. If you do qualify for this card, you are entitled to a range of discounts including on travel and course books. There is also a Graduate Extra card which you qualify for in the first year after graduating from university. For more information visit the NUS website which provides a range of other services and benefits. The NUS website also provides important information on your rights as a student and current campaigns.

The difficulties in comparing the cost of qualifications

Once you have established the cost of your qualification you might want to compare the cost of alternative qualifications. This can be very difficult as prices are not transparent in the qualifications market. Contrast the market for insurance. This market is dominated by price comparison websites which allow you, for example, to compare the cost of different types of car insurance based on information you put in about yourself. There is no equivalent price comparison website for qualifications in the UK. To overcome this you will have to invest some considerable additional time in listing the different costs of qualifications as the basis of a comparison. Remember to make sure you are comparing 'like for like' and that those prices cover the areas highlighted earlier in the chapter.

There are discussions currently taking place as to how to improve this situation and tools such as price comparison websites are being actively considered by the education authorities. Another issue being discussed is whether a tool could be developed showing what an average price should be for a particular type of qualification. This would be really useful to you as a consumer as you could quickly benchmark the value of particular qualifications that interest you.

There are some other potentially positive developments. Discussions between qualification developers and the education authorities are taking place about trying to give schools and colleges longer notice before increasing fees charged for qualifications. With longer notice periods you would be less likely to come across 'indicative prices' for qualifications. Other important areas under discussion are whether a common template could be used for displaying all price information with the aim of making this information more accessible. While all this is positive, the qualifications market, in its current form, lacks transparency. It remains difficult for you as a consumer to quickly establish whether the qualification you are considering is value for money.

Quality indicators

Remember that you are the consumer, and organisations are competing to sell you their qualifications. One result of the recent increase in tuition fees announced by most universities in England is that many higher education colleges are now beginning to offer cheaper, often more vocationally focused, degree programmes. This is an example of the market adapting to meet your demands as a consumer. It is important to be aware of the choices available before spending money on a qualification. The checklist below highlights what you have the right to expect from a high quality learning provider.

- ✓ Cost information should be easy to find and easy to understand.

- ✓ Cost information should be as accurate as possible for qualifications offered at future points in time.

- ✓ It should be clear how you pay for the qualification.

- ✓ There should be no hidden costs. All costs should be highlighted upfront, including any examination fees and potential fees for replacement certificates. There should be clear information on your right to cancel the qualification and the refunds you will be entitled to.

- ✓ It should be clear what funding, if any, you are entitled to.

- ✓ It should be clear if you are an EU or international student what impact that has on your tuition fees.

Funding

Funding is an important factor in choosing a qualification. The funding system can be complex, with its own terminology. There is a wide variety of schemes, which may or may not be relevant to you. This section outlines the main types of funding, provides a number of case studies and indicates where to go for information and advice.

Grant or bursary

A *grant* or *bursary* is money towards the costs of a qualification, which does not have to be paid back. Grants are available from local authorities in the UK, learning providers such as universities, colleges and schools, and many private organisations. To qualify for a grant you typically need to earn below a certain income threshold or have special learning requirements such as a disability. The type of grants and bursaries available depend on whether you are a full-time or part-time student. There are also important differences depending on whether you live in Scotland, England, Wales or Northern Ireland.

The management of these grants can vary depending on the type of qualification you do. An adult learner applying to do a vocational qualification at their local further education college would typically need to contact the college to discuss eligibility for financial support. *Discretionary Support Funds* for low-income adult learners are managed by schools and colleges. However a low-income adult learner applying for a maintenance grant for a degree could apply directly to a government agency for that grant. They could also apply to the university for further support in the form of a bursary.

Scholarship

A *scholarship* is an amount of money which you do not pay back. Scholarships are provided by learning providers, the government and many other organisations. They are designed to support learners in particular subjects, and are usually awarded to individuals with excellent academic attainment or to individuals in difficult financial circumstances. For example the National Scholarship Programme is available from Autumn 2012 to support students entering higher education. This government funded programme offers support to students in the form of a bursary or discounts on their course fees or accomodation. The BIS website is a good source of information.

Education loan

An *education loan* is an amount of money that you have to pay back, but often at favourable interest rates. There are different types of government loans in the UK designed specifically to help pay tuition fees, support professional development and help with the cost of living. In the UK, many learners take tuition fee loans to support them through university.

Other sources of funding

There is a wide range of other government, charity-based and private schemes making *education allowances* – for example, supporting disabled learners or learners with childcare costs. Learners can sometimes gain sponsorship to support the costs of a particular qualification. Some employers are willing to pay contributions towards the cost of a university degree. This is often contingent on you joining that organisation for a period of time after you have graduated. You need to contact employers to find out more about their *sponsorship* scheme.

Free qualifications

Some qualifications are free. If you are a learner under the age of 19 you do not pay for your qualifications. Adult learners are entitled to free literacy and numeracy courses. They also have entitlements to access free qualifications if they are taking their first level 2 qualification or, if they are under the age of 25, their first level 3 qualification. If you are claiming a benefit such as Jobseekers Allowance or Council Tax Benefit, many qualifications are free.

The aforementioned only applies to *publicly funded qualifications*. Publicly funded qualifications are qualifications which have been specifically approved by the governments in the UK as suitable for government funding. For example an adult learner in England, eligible on the grounds outlined above, would be funded by the Skills Funding Agency in taking one of their approved qualifications.

It is also important to note that the scope of a *free qualification* can vary depending on the category of learner you fall into. For example a young learner taking a GCSE will not pay any fees for that qualification whereas an adult learner taking their first level 2 qualification will not have to pay the tuition fees for that qualification but may have to pay any registration and examination fees. If you are unsure as to what concessions you qualify for, contact your learning provider.

The case studies below outline how you can access different types of funding.

Case study
Beth and the 14-19 Bursary Fund

Beth is 16 and plans to start her A levels. Beth is currently in care and is in very difficult financial circumstances. Beth contacts her local sixth form college to explain her circumstances. They confirm that she is eligible for a bursary of £1,200 a year in support of her A-level courses.

Case study
Graham improving his literacy skills

Graham's confidence has been undermined throughout his adult life by poor reading skills. Graham is determined to tackle this problem, but he is concerned by the potential cost of any qualification. Graham contacts the *Next Step careers advice service* and is told he has an entitlement to a free literacy course to help him deal with this problem. Graham enrols on a course with his local further education college. The college then secures funding for Graham from the Skills Funding Agency.

Case study
Bharat and a Professional and Career Development Loan

Bharat is looking to further develop his skills in management and is contemplating the NVQ Level 5 in Management. He has been unable to gain financial support from his employer and is looking for other sources of funding. One option for Bharat would be a *Professional and Career Development Loan*. He could qualify for a loan of between £300 and £10,000 for vocational or work-related learning (at the time of writing). This is a bank loan, so Bharat would need to repay the loan and pay an agreed rate of interest; however an attraction of the scheme is that the Young Persons Learning Agency will pay the interest on the loan while Bharat is taking the qualification and for the first month afterwards. The *Next Step careers advice service* would be able to provide Bharat with more information and an application pack.

Case study
Erin is budgeting for her bachelor's degree in engineering

Erin has accepted a place to study a bachelor's degree in engineering at university. Erin comes from a low-income family and is anxious about whether she can afford university. As a first step Erin needs to establish both the costs and potential sources of income. She analyses the financial information provided by her university and by UCAS. From this she establishes the costs of tuition fees, accommodation fees for her first year, and the likely cost of books and course materials. She also estimates the budget needed to cover food, bills and social expenses.

Erin plans to take on weekend work and has some savings; she has also identified a good student bank account. Her next step is to assess what loans, grants, scholarships or bursaries she is entitled to. She decides to take on a student loan. She establishes that she qualifies for a UK Government Higher Education Maintenance Grant and also for the university's own bursary scheme which is willing to provide an additional grant worth 50% of the government grant she is entitled to. In visiting the scholarships and funding section of her university's website she finds a number of scholarship schemes that she is eligible to apply for. While competition is tough, her strong academic background gives her a reasonable chance of success.

Funding information for higher education

For information on how to finance your studies in higher education the following organisations represent useful starting points:

- Each university will have comprehensive information on student finance.

- The UCAS service managing applications to universities also provides detailed information on student finance and advice on effective budget management.

- Each country in the UK has a student website which enables you to apply online for loans and grants, and provides comprehensive information on funding including sources of finance for disabled students. Depending on where you live you should visit Student Finance Wales, the Student Awards Agency in Scotland, Student Finance ni (Northern Ireland) or Student Finance England.

- If you are an EU student it is worth contacting the *Student Finance Services European Team* for information on student finance in the UK. Both European and international students can also find useful information through the organisations listed above. It should be noted that there are a number of scholarship schemes provided in the UK designed specifically for postgraduate international students.

Funding information for adult learners

Adult learners planning to study qualifications, outside of higher education, should go to the following organisations for information.

- Your local learning provider, such as a further education college, will be an excellent source of information and in many instances will be responsible for deciding on your eligibility for funding and/or allocating funds provided by other government agencies.

- If you live in Wales it is worth visiting the Guide to Funding for Adult Learners available through the Welsh Assembly government.

- If you live in Scotland it is worth visiting the *myworldofwork* website hosted by Skills Development Scotland.

- If you live in Northern Ireland it is worth visiting the *help with learning costs* section of the nidirect government services website.

- If you live in England it is worth visiting the funding information available through the Education and Learning section of the Directgov service and the funding section of the Next step careers advice service for adults.

Funding information for a young learner under the age of 19

In the first instance you should talk to your school or college. Wherever you live in the UK, it will be your school or college who can advise on your entitlements to funding. Schools and colleges often have discretionary support funds. These funds are prioritised for those in hardship. However there are important differences between how funding is managed across the UK. In Scotland, Wales and Northern Ireland you are entitled to apply for the government-funded Education Maintenance Allowance which entitles you to £30 of funding each week. In England this scheme has closed and has been replaced by the Discretionary Support Fund which is managed directly by your local school or college.

Where to go for more information about grants and scholarships

There is a wide range of grants and scholarships available in the UK. Specific organisations supporting areas such as sciences, humanities, art and dance all manage their own grant schemes. Many educational charities also provide funding for learners. To find out more a number of search options are suggested:

- The funding sections of your National Careers Advice Service. The Next Step Careers Advice Service in England has an A-Z of funding options for example.

- Other good sources of information include the Charities Digest, the Directory of Grant Making Trusts, the Education Grants Directory and the Grants Register.

- You can also search for a wide range of scholarships through the scholarship search engine powered by Hotcourses.

Other important questions about funding

You might have other important questions: for example, questions about help with the cost of childcare, about specific funds that support you to retrain if you are over 50, or about funding entitlements as a disabled learner. Your learning provider is a good source of information in the first instance. However, if you have yet to select a learning provider, the funding agencies listed above and the national careers services across the UK will also provide comprehensive advice and support. For more information about the national careers services in the UK go to Chapter 8.

Chapter 5
How to judge the quality of a qualification

This chapter:

→ Explains how to determine the quality of a qualification

→ Outlines four things to look for when choosing a qualification
- Good information
- Certification
- Regulation and quality assurance
- Reputation and employability

Some qualifications are of excellent quality and represent great value for money; other qualifications are of poor quality and not worth your time, effort or money. In Chapter 8 we highlight where to go to get advice in selecting high-quality qualifications. However it is important that you are clear in your own mind as to what constitutes quality in a qualification.

> **Case study**
> *Ravi searching for a high-quality web development qualification*
>
> Ravi is willing to spend a significant amount of money on a high quality web-development qualification. Ravi has done some initial research but is finding it hard to judge the quality of the qualifications available. The fact that Ravi is struggling is not his fault. He works full time and has a busy life. He plans to retrain while in full employment which is challenging for anyone. The qualification system is complex in the UK and it can be hard to get information. As a result it is all too easy to spend significant amounts of money on a qualification, based on incomplete information.
>
> Imagine if Ravi was buying a secondhand car and wanted to assess its quality. He would consider the reputation of the carmaker. He would buy a consumer magazine or go online to assess the consumer ratings given to different cars. He would also make a judgement on the reliability of the car dealership. A reputable dealer provides a guarantee, which is a promise to correct faults. Finally, his choice of car would be influenced by his own priorities. Is reliability more important to Ravi than a powerful engine, for example?

While it is much harder to assess the quality of a qualification than a car, there are important indicators of quality to look for as a consumer.

Good information

You need clear and accessible information when you are shopping for qualifications. Without this you cannot make an informed decision on which qualification is right for your needs. When you are looking at a qualification it should be straightforward to identify the following information.

Clear titles
The qualification title should clearly outline the main focus of the qualification. The unit or module titles should clearly identify the different subjects being covered. If the title of a qualification looks ambiguous, then avoid it, or at the very least pick up the phone and find out what the qualification aims to cover. Don't be afraid to challenge the title of a qualification.

Level
Does the qualification sit at a nationally recognised level in one of the UK's national qualifications frameworks? You need to have confidence that the qualification is at the appropriate level of difficulty for your needs. In researching qualifications, the qualification level is your initial and best indicator of difficulty.

What will the qualification lead to?
Does the qualification have clear links to progression? Within the information about the qualification there needs to be a clear statement explaining what the qualification leads to, or qualifies you for. If the qualification is a stepping stone towards qualifying you for a profession, it needs to be clear whether it partially or fully qualifies you for a particular profession, or for entry into further or higher education.

Is the qualification coherent?
This is a matter of judgement. Go into the structure of the qualification to make sure there are clearly defined subject areas that fit together coherently. If the structure seems confused, if there is duplication of content, or if the content covered does not meet your expectations, then avoid it.

The content of the qualification
It should not just be clear what subjects you are going to cover. It should also be clear what skills and knowledge are being developed and how they are going to be assessed. Does the qualification cover the skills that you think are going to be necessary for you as an employee? For vocational qualifications, one option is to visit the relevant Sector Skills Council (SSC) website to find out what skills employers look for. In addition if you are keen to work for a particular employer then have a

close look at their entry requirements and check that the qualification you are considering meets these requirements.

The length of the qualification
Is there clear information on the time commitment involved in taking the qualification? How many hours are you required to attend classes for? How many hours of your own study time will be required?

Will you get the flexibility you need?
What are the combinations of units or modules needed to achieve a qualification, and is there enough flexibility for you here? Does the qualification give you options to cover material quite different from the main focus of the qualification, if that is what you want? Does the qualification give you the option to interrupt your studies, or transfer your learning towards a different qualification?

Who is ultimately accountable for the qualification?
The qualification developer is ultimately responsible for your qualification, and this is not necessarily the organisation that teaches you. You need to be aware of the identity of the qualification developer even if you are unlikely to have much day-to-day contact with this organisation.

Cost
Is there clear information on the cost of the qualification? The previous chapter describes the information that should be available here.

Some of this information might take some further research but it is your right to obtain this information without too much effort. If you cannot, the organisation you are dealing with is not providing information in a transparent manner.

> **Example**
> *Richmond upon Thames College and its presentation of information*
>
> A learner searching for qualifications offered by Richmond upon Thames College is presented with a commendable level of detail on each course. In selecting a particular qualification, they will first be presented with the fundamentals – title, level, start date, attendance days and times, and examining body (awarding organisation). The

course details are then outlined, followed by sections on 'who the course is for' 'am I qualified' and 'what the course will cover'.

The learning outcomes for the qualification are defined in a section entitled 'what can I do as a result of this course.' Information is provided on how the course will be taught and importantly 'how will I know I am progressing and how is the course assessed'. There is also a section of information which outlines how you can get your views across, as a learner on the course, and about 'where the course will lead to.' Finally, detailed information is provided on fees and concessions and how and when to enrol. This level of course information represents excellent practice.

Certification

A qualification certificate is a very important document. It is your evidence that you have achieved the qualification. It is the responsibility of the qualification developer to issue you with a qualification certificate. Best practice in terms of managing and producing certificates is outlined below. This is what the education authorities in the UK expect of a good certificate:

- Your name should be clearly written.

- The full qualification title and level should be stated.

- The mark/grade/result you gained should be stated.

- It should carry the logo of the qualification developer, and of the qualification's regulator, if applicable.

- It might reference the learning provider that delivered the qualification to you, but this is not mandatory.

- It should have some form of unique identification. Different systems are used by different qualification developers, but this might include a *Unique Learner Number* (ULN).

- Some qualification developers will also provide you with a supporting *transcript* which provides further detail on your achievement, for example the detailed marks or results you gained for the individual units.

- The qualification developer should send you the certificate within a reasonable timeframe.

- If you lose or damage your certificate, you have a right to expect a replacement certificate or at least a certifying statement of results from the qualification developer. The charge for this should not be excessive.

- From 2012 all qualification certificates in the UK, which again are subject to the scrutiny of the qualification regulator, will need to make a reference to the European Qualifications Framework (EQF), a referencing system being currently rolled out across the European Union. For more information on this initiative please go to Chapter 9.

Regulated and quality-assured

An important consideration for you is whether your qualification is nationally-recognised and regulated by one of the education authorities in the UK.

Example
Regulation in the insurance industry

If you are buying car insurance or home insurance your rights are protected as a consumer. You have the right to be told exactly what you are buying and not to discover any hidden clauses or hidden charges. You have the right to cancel your insurance policy. You have the right to a high level of customer service and the right to clearly outlined procedures if you have a complaint. Your rights are safeguarded in two important ways:

1. **By a regulator** A regulator is an organisation responsible for ensuring that consumers get a fair deal. The regulator protects your rights. If a problem arises with your insurance and you feel

the insurance company has treated you unfairly, you can take your grievance to the regulator.

2. **By the management of the insurance companies themselves**
   They are competing for your business and are trying to meet and exceed the requirements outlined by the regulator.

The qualifications system works in the same way. The highest status qualifications in the UK are recognised by either a regulator or by a professional body. These organisations safeguard your rights as a learner. They make checks on the quality of both the organisations that develop and deliver qualifications to you. If a qualification is regulated you can expect a certain level of quality in how a qualification is made, how it is assessed, and how it is taught. The regulators also work to ensure that the standard of a qualification remains constant over time.

These regulatory bodies are also there to protect your rights if something goes wrong that cannot be dealt with by the qualification developer and learning provider. This means you have the comfort of knowing a regulator will help protect you if a problem arises. Your rights as a learner are more secure where they are enforced in this way. These rights rarely need to be enforced but are there 'just in case'. When you research a qualification, determining whether that qualification is regulated is an important step in being reassured that the qualification is of high quality.

Does it matter if a qualification is not regulated?
Many qualifications in the UK are not regulated. These qualifications may be of excellent quality and subject to robust quality assurance. These organisations may have no need to be regulated because their brand and reputation are so strong.

> **Example**
> *Microsoft: a global reputation for excellence in learning*
>
> Microsoft has a strong global reputation for certificating IT professionals. More than 4.5 million IT professionals have gained Microsoft certificates validating their skills in particular IT functions. Microsoft has its own professional community of successful learners, which

provides a range of benefits. It also runs IT academies which deliver training in a wide variety of forms.

Microsoft calls its qualifications *certifications* and operates its own level system for certifications starting at Associate level, moving through different levels to Microsoft-certified Professional Developer, and finally to the highest level of a Microsoft-certified Architect. Their examinations are subject to robust quality assurance procedures and a comprehensive system of internal examination regulations. These Microsoft qualifications clearly demonstrate the excellent practice that can exist outside the scope of national regulatory bodies.

However, the unregulated qualifications market does inevitably have pockets of poor practice, where 'qualification cowboys' peddle poor quality qualifications. An example of this is the recent proliferation of organisations selling singing, dancing and drama qualifications, promising future success to young people. There have been concerns in the national media about the claims made by these unregulated qualification providers in encouraging young people to buy their qualifications on the basis of unrealistic claims that they will lead to TV stardom.

Organisations can also be disingenuous as to whether their qualifications are nationally recognised by the relevant regulatory body. There are cases of qualification developers and learning providers falsely presenting the status of their qualifications. You need to be clear as a consumer that a qualification is either recognised or not recognised and there is no scope for ambiguity in this area. A master's degree in business administration, for example, is highly valued precisely because it is very hard for organisations to gain the official recognition to develop and deliver this level and type of qualification. An organisation which claims to offer 'undergraduate level' or 'master's level' qualifications which are not recognised by regulatory bodies is to be avoided.

How can you tell if a qualification is regulated?
There are a number of ways you can tell if a qualification is regulated.

- Qualification developers should always declare if their qualification is positioned in a regulated framework. This is in their self interest because it highlights the quality of their qualification. Note that they might describe their qualifications as *accredited*. This is another way of saying the qualification is regulated. If a qualification has gained accredited status it will have been through lots of different checks to make sure it is ready for you to take as a learner.

- If a qualification title has a national level this will be referenced in its title.

- A qualification title uses BA, MA or a number of the other specific naming conventions used by universities and other institutes of higher education.

- If an organisation is recognised or accredited by a regulatory body it will highlight this information as a mark of quality. The mark or logo of the regulatory body should be easy to find on their webpage. Typically the logo of the regulatory body is positioned at the bottom of the homepage. The different regulatory bodies working across the UK are referenced in Annex4.

Further checks on the regulated status of a qualification

If you are unsure whether a qualification is regulated you can conduct a number of further searches. For national qualifications outside of higher education you can visit the register of regulated qualifications for England, Wales and Northern Ireland which is jointly maintained by the following regulatory bodies, Ofqual (The Office of Qualifications and Examinations) in England, CCEA (Council for the Curriculum, Examinations and Assessment) in Northern Ireland and the Welsh Assembly government in Wales. This register lists thousands of nationally recognised qualifications, outside of higher education, that have been checked and approved by these regulatory bodies as being of sufficient quality for you to study. In Scotland, SQA accreditation accredits vocational qualifications offered across Scotland. These accredited qualifications can be searched for through the SQA website.

Universities and other institutes of higher education (certain colleges for example) are given the right to award different types of degrees by an Act of Parliament or by Royal charter. This gives them the status as *recognised bodies*, which are then quality assured by the Quality Assurance Agency (QAA). If you visit the QAA website you will find a list of these organisations operating in the UK.

There are a number of important accreditation and inspection schemes operating across the UK. Publicly funded schools and colleges and a wide range of other learning providers are inspected by Government Inspectorates; Ofsted, in England, ETINI, (The Education and Training Inspectorate Northern Ireland), ESTYN (Her Majesty's Inspectorate for Education and Training in Wales) and Education Scotland. These organisations all make their inspection reports on learning providers publicly available on their websites.

The British Council through its Accreditation UK scheme accredits learning providers offering English Language courses and the British Accreditation Council accredits a range of private colleges. Most independent schools in the UK are members of the Independent Schools Council (ISC) and subject to regular inspections from the Independent Schools Inspectorate (ISI). Again these organisations provide a list of their accredited learning providers on their websites.

Reputation and employability

The reputation of a qualification is important. However good a qualification is, if it is poorly perceived by employers, university admission tutors and other people making decisions, then you will be at a disadvantage if you proceed with that qualification. These are the key steps in establishing the reputation of your qualification.

The Sector Skills Council website is a good starting point for determining the status of a qualification within a particular industry. Each Sector Skills Council website will have a section outlining what qualifications are required to progress in their industry. This helps you establish what skills are needed and what types of qualifications are respected in a particular sector.

Take the time to research what prior qualifications, if any, employers or learning providers view as important or indeed essential, if you want to work or study with them. An internet search should reveal any news headlines about a qualification and how it is viewed in the media. Finally make sure you talk to the people that matter. Talk to teachers, careers advisers, admission tutors and recruitment managers for employers. Find out what qualifications they view as of high quality and what qualifications they view as of poor quality.

Determining the employability of a qualification

Qualifications increase your chances of getting a job and also increase the salary gained over your lifetime. The Office of National Statistics say that graduates, for example, earned an average of £12,000 a year more than non-graduates over the past decade.

Different qualifications will have a different impact on your employability. Some qualifications focus specifically on the skills you need in a particular workplace, and would score very highly on an employability rating. An Apprenticeship in Engineering is focused on developing the precise skills required for that industry.

Other qualifications will have less immediate benefit in getting a job; others still might be quite negatively perceived by employers. The CBI, which is the UK's main lobbying group for business, has frequently criticised the failure of many qualifications to develop the skills needed in the work place – literacy, numeracy, effective communication skills, team working and professionalism.

If you are using a qualification to gain the skills needed for the workplace, good research is required to identify both the reputation of the qualification amongst employers, but also to make your own judgement as to whether the qualification is developing the skills you require. You can make this judgement by reviewing the knowledge and skills outlined in the page of course detail on the qualification. In addition there are some powerful tools you can use.

The *Bestcourses4me* service enables you to assess the benefits of taking a particular qualification by showing you the link between what other people have studied and their employment records afterwards. So, if you want to study a graduate level qualification in Maths, you run a search and a range of statistics will be generated which show you your likely hourly pay and how this will change over your lifetime. Statistics also show the likelihood of you gaining employment in this area.

In establishing how employable a qualification will make you, careful research is required. It is easy to be deterred by the general reputation of a particular subject. However, proper research into the reputation enjoyed by individual courses can unearth a very different picture, as the case study below demonstrates.

> **Example**
> *Bournemouth University and the international reputation of its media courses*
>
> Media qualifications have for decades been perceived as 'soft options' both as entry qualifications for university and as university degrees. This prejudice can obscure the international reputation for excellence achieved by some media courses offered in the UK.
>
> The Media School at Bournemouth University offers a range of postgraduate and undergraduate courses in Media Production, Journalism & Communication, Computer Animation and Corporate & Marketing Communications. The Media School and in particular its National Centre for Computer Animation has achieved an outstanding level of success. A report published by NESTA (the National Endowment for Science, Technology and Art) in February 2011 reported that nearly '50% of graduates working in the film, visual effects or video games industries in the UK come from Bournemouth University'. Another impressive fact is that 50 Bournemouth graduates and former academic colleagues worked on the set of the film Avatar (source Bournemouth University website).

Quality indicators

A high quality qualification has the following characteristics:

- ✓ There is clear information on the qualification's content, structure, cost, length, level and what it enables learners to do.

- ✓ Learners are given a uniquely identifiable certificate which clearly presents their achievements.

- ✓ The qualification is subject to some form of regulation or quality assurance. If a qualification is regulated this gives a basic guarantee of quality and numerous safeguards. However, it should be noted that many high profile qualifications are not regulated but are subject to rigorous internal quality checks.

- ✓ The qualification has a good reputation with the people that matter.

- ✓ If relevant, the qualification develops the skills needed to gain employment in today's workplace.

Chapter 6
How to judge the quality of assessment

This chapter:

- → Explains why it is important to understand how a qualification is assessed

- → Highlights the importance of understanding the practical details supporting an assessment

- → Establishes how you can be confident that you will be assessed fairly

- → Describes how your issues and questions on assessments should be managed

The results you gain in a qualification can change your life. So you need clear information about how you will be assessed, before starting a qualification; the type of assessment used might even influence your choice of qualification. The quality of the information you receive on assessment and how any special requirements, issues or questions will be managed also provides an insight into the quality of the learning provider itself. Of course, there is a level of detail involved in the assessment process that is not relevant to you as consumer, but a broad understanding of the process is essential for you as a consumer.

What do you need to know about assessment?

Before starting a qualification you need to know what content is being assessed and how the assessment will be conducted. You need to know how you will be graded.

What will you be assessed on?
This information is usually available in the assessment criteria of the qualification. This framework gives focus to your study and revision. It also provides a benchmark against which you can judge the effectiveness of the teaching you receive.

The assessment criteria link directly to the learning outcomes in a qualification. The *learning outcomes* state the knowledge and skills that need to be developed in each unit. The *assessment criteria* outline what evidence is required as proof of your learning.

What assessment methods will be used?
Once you have established what is being assessed it is important to establish how you will be assessed. A good learning provider will make this clear. For example, what proportion of the qualification is assessed by a written exam and what proportion of the qualification is assessed by coursework? Will the assessment be based on multiple-choice questions or open-ended questions? What types of evidence will meet the assessment criteria?

Exhibit 6 The relationship between learning outcomes and assessment criteria

Learning outcomes	Assessment criteria
Know the origin of banks	• Describe the origins of banks • Describe how the origins have a direct impact on the role and purpose of banks today • Describe the role of confidence in the banks by their customers and the wider world
Know the functions of banks	• Describe how banks make profits • Describe why banks take deposits • Describe why banks lend money • Describe the principles of the monetary transfer system
Understand the need for other sources of finance	• Explain how banks rely upon liquidity for their survival • Discuss why a range of sources of finance are necessary for banks

Source: Edexcel's Level 3 BTEC Advanced Diploma in Banking and Finance Unit 1 The Nature of Banking

Case study
Karl establishing what evidence is acceptable for his portfolio

Karl is doing a level 2 qualification in Teamwork and Communication Skills. He is highly motivated and wants to produce a creative and interesting portfolio which clearly meets the assessment criteria. Karl sits down with his supervisor and talks through the types of evidence that will be acceptable. He is considering videoing a short play on the problem of bullying. His supervisor, after double checking with the awarding organisation, confirms that this would be considered favourably.

How will the assessment be graded?

What grading system and conventions will be used? Many learners undertake a qualification without this knowledge. A number of different grading systems are used across the UK. Some examples are described below.

- Many bachelors degrees use 1st, 2:1, 2:2, 3rd and fail.

- Many masters degrees and some vocational qualifications use distinction, merit, pass or fail or a variation of those levels. Note that 'credit' is sometimes used instead of merit.

- Many vocational qualifications simply use pass or fail.

- 14-19 qualifications, such as GCSEs and A levels, use a grading scale from A* to E in the case of A levels and A* to G in the case of GCSEs, with U as ungraded.

- Some qualifications, such as the International English Language Testing System (IELTS), give you a score on a specific scale. For example IELTS will give you a points score out of nine.

You need to know what distinguishes different levels of achievement. This information is made explicit in the *marking criteria* or *marking scheme*. A good learning provider will make their marking criteria publicly available and spend time in class familiarising you with this information. Understanding the marking criteria enables you to judge your own progress and have informed discussions with your teachers. The need for clarity about marking criteria applies just as much to apparently subjective judgements, such as the quality of an art portfolio in an arts degree.

A good learning provider will use a range of techniques to ensure you develop a robust understanding of the assessment criteria and mark schemes used in the qualification. For example they might ask you to mark a fellow learner's practice paper (a process called *peer assessment*) or ask you to mark your practice paper (a process called *self assessment*).

You should also be given clear guidance in preparation for each individual assessment. This could include information on how different questions are weighted – what allocation of marks is given to different questions – and detail on how those questions are marked. For example, in a maths examination you need to know if showing your workings will gain marks, even if your final answer is incorrect. This type of information informs your exam strategy.

In written assignments, you need to know the word limits and conventions relating to footnotes, references and bibliographies. If you are producing a dissertation you should get support from your tutor to make sure your work meets the assessment criteria.

> **Case study**
> *Janet downloading the qualification specification*
>
> Janet is considering doing a BTEC Foundation Diploma in Art and Design. She has found some good information on the website of her local learning provider but wants further detail on assessment. Janet has established that Edexcel is the awarding organisation responsible for the development and award of the BTEC by finding their name in the title of the qualification on the Edexcel website the specification gives information on the aims and structure of the qualification, an overview of the assessment and grading, and how previous relevant learning is managed. There is also information on how the assessment is quality assured, how reasonable adjustments and special considerations are managed, and detailed information on the learning outcomes, and assessment criteria in each unit together with what evidence is acceptable in meeting those criteria.

In establishing how your qualification is marked you need to know how your results are added together to form your overall grade. For many qualifications you will gain your unit results as you progress through your studies and you need to be clear on whether you are on track for your overall mark. You may need to know whether it is possible to pass the qualification even if you fail one unit.

Pass rates

A good learning provider will be keen to publish results showing how previous learners have performed in the qualification. Look in their marketing brochures or on their websites where this information should be prominently displayed. If you struggle to find this information, it might be because the learning provider has poor pass rates.

> **Case study**
> *Paul seeking more precise information about how he is being marked*
>
> Paul is in his second year of university studying history and politics. He is frustrated with the last three marks he gained in his written assignments. In each of these assignments he scored a percentage mark in the high 50s, which is just below the level of a 2:1. Because he wants to achieve a 2:1 degree he decides to take some active steps. As a first step he downloads the assessment criteria for history and politics from the university website and identifies the knowledge and skills required to gain a 2:1. He books some additional time with his seminar tutors and gets their feedback on how he can improve. Finally he enrols on a number of study skills workshops provided by the university that focus on developing research skills, on clearly structuring written arguments, and on improving writing style.

Resits, resubmissions and retaking units

The learning provider should have clear rules about whether you can resit your examinations or resubmit your assignments and how many times you can do this. You should know what impact failing any one unit has on your continued progress and what the policy is with regards to repeating units if you are dissatisfied with your performance or fail to reach the standard required. It should be noted that not all qualifications offer resits and it is worth establishing this in your initial investigations. Be aware that where resits are offered there might well be an additional cost involved. It is worth considering that a university might raise their entry requirements if you decide to resit the qualification.

The importance of understanding the practical details

To maximise your chances of success you need to make sure you take account of any detailed rules relating to an assessment. For example, check if a maths exam allows the use of a calculator. A good learning provider will give you the information you need well in advance of the assessment.

Dates and times

A learning provider should give, well in advance, precise information on the dates and times of examinations and the submission dates for written assessments or portfolios. You should also be given the dates for any *mock* or practice exams or draft submission points for written assignments. This information helps you plan your study.

You need to know when and how you will get your results after taking an assessment. This date might influence when you apply for jobs or when you plan your holiday. A good learning provider will always keep to their published timescales in issuing results. Delays can only be justified in exceptional circumstances.

You should be given clear information on the length of the exam and the amount of time allocated for each section or question. This information helps you develop an effective strategy for taking the exam.

Support
You need to know how much help and advice you can expect from your teacher in preparing for an exam or in developing a written assignment or portfolio. As a consumer you need to get the most from your teachers and to be clear on what they can and cannot do for you.

Current debates
Recent abuses, and the move away from coursework

While assessment systems in the UK are generally robust, and teaching is highly professional, there are isolated incidents of teachers who provide too much assistance. There have been cases of teachers giving learners the actual exam questions during practice sessions or allowing learners to correct mistakes at the end of an examination. There have been other incidents involving portfolios and written assessments where it has been suspected that a teacher or family member has done some of the work submitted.

Increasingly, assessed work is either done sitting in an exam hall or in controlled conditions. Assessment in controlled conditions allows you to produce a piece of work over a given period of time, under supervision, and the work cannot be taken home. This movement towards assessment in controlled conditions is most evident in qualifications such as A levels and GCSEs. *Coursework* remains an accepted method of assessment in universities.

The exam rules on the day
The way in which the exam will be managed needs to be clearly outlined. You need to know what you can and cannot do. Can you bring a dictionary into an English Language examination or a calculator into a statistics exam? Are you allowed a toilet break? What should you do if you finish early or arrive late? What stationery can you bring? What happens if you make a mistake on the paper? Can you bring annotated text books to an English Literature exam? What constitutes cheating or misconduct also needs to be clearly defined so you don't accidentally break the rules.

All of these questions require answers and a good learning provider should inform you of the rules well in advance of the day of the exam, giving you the time to prepare effectively.

Serious cases of misconduct might involve *plagiarism*, collusion between learners in sharing answers to exam questions or, in some cases, the impersonation of another learner. You also need to be clear on the penalties for the late submission of assessments and also the consequences of deliberate or accidental misconduct in a formal exam.

Assessment that is fair and accurate

You need to be able to trust that your work will be marked fairly. How can you gain this confidence? Below, we describe the features of a rigorous assessment system. As a qualifications consumer you do not need to know the fine detail of how you are assessed, but it is important to have a general awareness of what constitutes good practice.

In the area of assessment the distinction between the role of the qualification developer and learning provider is important. Where these organisations are different, it is the qualification developer who is accountable for the standard of assessment. It is the qualification developer who will design the assessment and quality assure the marking of the assessments.

Does the assessment properly measure your knowledge and skills?
You should feed confident that the assessment allows you to demonstrate the full breadth of knowledge and skills covered in the unit.

Assessment questions should be clearly structured, free from errors, and should enable you to effectively demonstrate what you have learnt.

The assessment should also provide sufficient scope for differentiation on the basis of ability. Taken to an extreme, a maths test which simply asks learners to add 2 + 2 is not providing sufficient scope to assess different levels of mathematical ability. At the other extreme, a 10,000 word written assignment would be a very unrealistic method of assessment for a level 1 qualification in Adult Literacy, both in terms of its level of difficulty and the time it would take. The assessment needs to be sufficiently detailed and challenging to enable assessors to differentiate between excellent, good, average and inadequate answers.

Preparation and feedback

A good learning provider will try to ease the burden placed on you as a learner and on the assessors marking your work. This involves giving you enough time to prepare for an exam and also giving the assessor enough time to mark your work before results are due. If you are told that you have an examination the following day, this is clearly poor practice. Likewise, if your assessors are only given one day to mark 60 written assignments this is also poor practice.

You need to be given appropriate and timely feedback on any assessments. The nature and extent of assessor feedback also needs to be clear to you. If you are being informally assessed midway through your unit, you need enough time to consider the feedback and make any necessary changes to your approach.

The accuracy of marking

What constitutes accuracy depends on context and can vary depending on the type of assessment you have taken. In a multiple-choice assessment you need to be confident that the assessor will not make mistakes, even when the marking process just involves checking for the right answer. In a written assignment you need to be confident the assessor has a strong understanding of the marking scheme and is able to effectively mark your work against this scheme.

Current debates
Errors in GCSE and A-level papers

In July 2011 the UK's five largest awarding organisations setting GCSEs and A levels issued a statement on the summer's examinations, saying: 'This summer, ten examination questions contained an error. Although this is a small proportion of the more than 60,000 questions set across over 5,000 papers, we know that any error in such a vital process is unacceptable. We regret that these errors have occurred and we apologise to all students affected.' It is estimated that these errors affected over 250,000 learners, many of whom were dependent on these grades to secure university places. In reality a small number of mistakes is inevitable, but they can have a very damaging effect on wider public confidence. Qualification developers need to demonstrate both how they will manage the affected learners – by awarding full marks for the problem questions, for example – and also how they will mitigate against the risks of significant errors in future exam papers.

You need to be confident that the judgements made by your assessor will be consistent with the judgement of the other assessors marking the same qualifications across the country. Furthermore you need to know that these judgements are consistent over time. This consistency in assessment practice is another way of describing the 'standard' of a qualification, which we defined in Chapter 1.

The quality of your assessors
You have a right to expect that the people assessing your work have the necessary expertise, the right qualifications, and have been given adequate training to properly assess your work.

A good learning provider will not simply hand their assessors the marking criteria to read. They will spend time supporting their assessors in developing a deeper understanding of the assessment criteria and marking scheme through workshops, discussions of sample answers, the marking of dummy assessment papers and the design of real or practice assessment papers.

Even very experienced assessors or examiners can make slightly different judgements on the same piece of work. While these differences of opinion will always exist, robust systems need to be in place to minimise differences.

There are lots of different terms used to describe this process of checking the quality of marking. You might come across the terms *moderation*, *verification* and *standardisation*. Moderation and verification activities ensure that a certain sample, say 10%, of the marked work of a particular assessor, is cross checked by someone else, usually a senior examiner or team leader. This sample will include the work of strong, average and weak candidates, work which is considered borderline (between two grades or two levels) and work which is considered to fail the standard. Any differences in interpretation of the mark scheme can then be reviewed.

You might also come across the terms *internal* and *external* moderators, verifiers or examiners. An internal verifier is typically a teacher at the learning provider or at a neighbouring learning provider who is checking the marking of his colleagues. An external verifier is usually employed by the qualification developer, if different to the learning provider. This external person conducts a further series of checks on the work reviewed by the internal verifier.

The people assessing your work should have no conflict of interest, be objective in assessing your work and have no bias for or against you or your place of study. A good learning provider or qualification developer will run checks against their assessors to ensure there is no conflict of interest.

Transparent decision making
The policies and procedures relating to assessment decisions should be available for you to see. For example, it might reassure you to know that your scripts are anonymised (your names are removed from assignments) to prevent bias or that your assessments are going to be *double marked* by an independent assessor. It should be clear how borderline cases are managed and also how disagreements between markers are resolved.

Cheating

A good learning provider will invest in systems that detect cheating and have clear procedures for managing any incidents. Many universities are investing in sophisticated software packages such as *turnitin,* which can detect incidents of internet-based plagiarism. They should also have confidential procedures enabling you to report any suspected incidents of cheating amongst your fellow learners.

The application of special considerations

The learning provider, often working to the rules outlined by the qualification developer, should make special considerations in appropriate cases. Special considerations were defined in Chapter 1, as ensuring learners are treated fairly in the event they miss an exam or their performance is affected by, for example, a family bereavement.

In this event the learning provider should make alternative arrangements, or if resitting an exam is not possible, they need to ensure that marks given to the learner take into consideration their personal circumstances. In some cases where a learner misses an exam, an approximate mark is given based on their previous performance.

A good learning provider will clearly define what warrants special considerations and will apply their rules consistently. For example, while a serious family illness might well warrant a special consideration, it is unlikely that an illness of a pet will be considered a valid reason for missing an exam. Special considerations should be applied consistently from one learner to the next. Note that special considerations are sometimes referred to as extenuating circumstances in higher education.

Assessments in different languages

In certain situations you might have the right to take an assessment in a different language. For example as a learner in Wales you might have the entitlement to conduct your assessment in the Welsh language. It is always worth discussing your rights in this area with the learning provider before starting on a qualification.

Security

Any work you produce for an assessment should be securely kept and be given some form of unique identification so it will not be confused with the work of someone else. The learning provider should have contingency plans in the event your assessments are damaged or lost by an act of nature such as fire or flood. The learning provider should also have a clear policy on the length of time it keeps your work.

Reasonable adjustments

If you have a disability you need to be aware of your rights in being able to access qualifications. It is not acceptable for a learning provider to say that because you are hearing impaired there is no point you studying a qualification in German. This constitutes discrimination. All nationally-recognised qualifications have a legal duty not to discriminate against someone with any form of special need or disability. This informs both the initial design of assessments – for example, what type of questions are asked in an assessment and also how the assessment is managed on the day.

A learning provider, often working to rules set out by the qualification developer, has to make reasonable adjustments to enable you to be assessed in a way that takes into consideration your particular requirements. What this organisation cannot do is give you an unfair advantage over other learners. They need to balance making reasonable adjustments, which enable you to access the assessment, with ensuring the standard of the qualification.

A good example occurs in judging a portfolio of work which relies very heavily on the use of *witness statements*. Witness statements are often used in vocational qualifications as evidence that a learner has met the assessment requirements. They are particularly useful if the learner has special requirements that prevent them producing their own write ups of a task. However there is a danger that the learner's portfolio becomes too reliant on witness statements and includes no material directly produced by the learner. In this situation it becomes difficult to judge whether that learner has met the assessment criteria.

How your questions and issues on assessment should be managed

Given the importance of assessment you might well have questions that need to be answered. If an assessment is poorly managed you could well have grounds for making a complaint.

Customer services and complaints

A good learning provider will have clear procedures and systems in place for managing any issues, complaints or questions you have with the assessment of your qualification. These procedures should include a time limit within which you can expect a response and will explain what happens next if you remain dissatisfied.

The right to appeal your mark

You are entitled to *appeal* against an assessment decision you disagree with. Procedures should be clearly outlined explaining how you, or a teacher on your behalf, can ask for your assessment to be remarked. It should be clear how to make an initial request for a remark and how long the appeal process will take. Your results should be reviewed by someone who is independent, unbiased, and who was not involved in the initial marking of your work.

The different stages of the appeal process should be clearly outlined on the website of the learning provider. It should be noted that in many cases the remarking of an assessment will be the responsibility of the qualification developer and not the learning provider who taught you the qualification.

> **Case study**
> *Chris challenging his maths A-level result*
>
> Chris gained a B in his maths A level which meant he missed meeting the entry requirements of his first choice university by one grade. Chris was surprised by his result as he felt he performed well in the examinations. After discussing his results with his parents, teachers and school exam officers he asks his school to submit an *enquiry about results (EAR)* to the awarding organisation. Because Chris has a university place depending on the outcome of the results he can

submit a Priority Service 2 Enquiry which will fast track the review of his marks.

Chris's exam papers are reviewed by a senior examiner but the marks are not changed. Chris remains dissatisfied and reviews his remaining options. As a next step Chris can ask his head teacher to take forward an appeal with the awarding organisation, appealing the review conducted by the senior examiner. If this is unsuccessful he has exhausted the appeal process. In this situation he can chose another university with his current grades or resit his maths A level which would delay starting his university studies.

Quality indicators

As a learner what matters most is the quality of information you are given on assessments. Most of the time this is all you need to know. However, in certain circumstances you might also need or want to investigate the accuracy and fairness of your assessment. High-quality assessment processes have the following characteristics.

- ✓ There is clear information on the assessment criteria, the methods of assessment and the grade scheme if relevant.

- ✓ There is clear information on pass rates.

- ✓ There is detailed and practical information on the rules and requirements supporting examinations and on other forms of assessment.

- ✓ The learning provider ensures that learners fully understand the assessment criteria and are given adequate time to prepare.

- ✓ The learning provider has clear procedures and effectively manages assessment questions, issues or appeals.

- ✓ The assessment is fair and accurate. This means the assessment effectively measures the relevant knowledge and skills at the right level of difficulty. It also means the marking is consistent and accurate primarily because the people marking assessments have the necessary training and expertise.

- ✓ The assessments are accessible for disabled learners.
- ✓ Assessment papers and completed assessments are kept securely.
- ✓ There are effective systems in place to prevent cheating.

Chapter 7
How to judge the quality of a learning provider

This chapter:

→ Explains how to determine the quality of a learning provider

→ Identifies the key areas that the qualifications consumer should look at, including:
- ✓ The quality of the information provided by the learning provider
- ✓ The quality of resources and the quality of the teaching and learning support
- ✓ The provision for learners with particular needs
- ✓ The customer service and the processes for managing complaints

→ Shows how to utilise inspection reports and other sources of information on the quality of a learning provider

The term *learning provider* encompasses all the different places you can study a qualification including schools, colleges, universities, prisons, employers, online and distance learning providers. This chapter explains the general indicators of quality which apply to all learning providers. Some of these indicators will help you decide on which learning provider to choose. Others will outline what you should expect on starting a qualification.

Robust entry requirements and application procedures

The entry requirements and *application procedures* should always be clear and easy to understand. As a consumer you need confidence that your application will be reviewed fairly, consistently and professionally. Note that many learning providers, such as further education colleges, refer to their '*admissions process*' or 'enrolment' rather than their 'application process'. These terms are interchangeable although sometimes the term enrolment is used specifically to describe joining a course with no entry requirements.

Clear information on how to apply

This information should outline what qualifications and/or work experience you are required to have and should be sufficiently detailed for you to determine your eligibility. This information will typically be found on the website of the learning provider.

- ✓ You need to find out what the application process will involve.

- ✓ What information about yourself do you need to submit?

- ✓ Are references required?

- ✓ Do you need to write a personal statement, if so what should this cover?

- ✓ Will you be interviewed, if so what will this interview involve?

- ✓ Will you have to take an entrance exam, if so what will be the focus of the exam?

Specific qualifications, for example qualifications in art and design, might require you to bring your portfolio of artwork to the interview.

The timescales for the application process need to be clearly outlined. What is the deadline for applications? When and where will interviews take place? Some learning providers run enrolment evenings that allow you to find out more about a qualification and sign up at the same time; the dates for these should be clearly specified. It should also be clear when you will be informed if you have been successful in securing a place.

There should be specific information supporting applications from EU or international students, covering visa requirements, the level of English language required and how interviews will be managed. The British Council provides information for international students wanting to apply to study in the UK. As international students you might also need to establish the equivalency between your qualifications and the entry requirements to study in the UK. The British Council provides good advice, however the most authoritative organisation in this area is UK NARIC. More information on the role of UK NARIC is provided in Chapter 9.

A learning provider should provide frequent updates on the availability of places. Some qualifications are offered continuously through the year, but when a qualification offered at a particular point in the year is full, this information should be available on the website.

Points of contact should be provided for questions you have on the application process. A good learning provider will provide a phone number for you to contact; they might also provide a set of frequently asked questions.

Example
The role of UCAS in managing applications

> For certain qualifications you do not need to apply directly to the learning provider but can apply through an admissions service such as UCAS (Universities and Colleges Admissions Service) or UKPASS (The UK Postgraduate Application and Statistical Service). These

services centrally manage applications for universities and other institutes of higher education. There is usually a small charge for these services. UCAS, for example, allows you to apply online for five courses across different learning providers. It allows you to manage and track your applications and accept and decline offers. You will need to work to the timescales outlined by UCAS. It operates three deadlines for course applications in October, January and March. UCAS also operates a clearing service. If you have been unsuccessful in meeting the grades for your original university offers, did not receive any offers or declined the offers you did receive, you can go through the clearing system. This system matches up learners who have yet to find a place with universities who still have places available on particular courses. This service is available each year after exam results are published in August. Visit the UCAS website for more information on this process.

The management of your application

How your application is managed provides an early insight into the quality of the learning provider. A learning provider should always meet its published timelines in processing your application. If you are required to attend an interview, you have a right to expect a high level of professionalism in the type and manner of questions asked.

It is good practice to require you to provide original versions of your certificates to authenticate the claims made in your application. A diligent learning provider will also quickly contact the referees you provide on your application form. If your application is not properly scrutinised you are entitled to question the professionalism of the learning provider.

The quality of the information provided by the learning provider

How the learning provider presents itself on its website, in its brochure and other marketing material helps you judge its quality. A high quality organisation will present itself professionally, but also accurately. If you come across a learning provider that seems to be making bold claims always try and conduct further research to validate this information.

Information on the services provided by the learning provider

A school, college or university is not just a place to learn. It may provide a wide range of extracurricular activities, such as trips, social activities and sports. It can be a place where people go to eat, drink coffee and meet with friends. The wider experience provided by a learning provider may be important in deciding where to go and study. If a learning provider does not provide any information about its extracurricular activities and wider resources then you are entitled to doubt if it has any.

> **Example**
> *West Thames College and what it offers learners*
>
> The West Thames College, in its website and publications, places a strong value on the importance of the wider community it offers learners. The website provides a detailed events calendar outlining fresher fairs (opportunities for new starters to find out about life at the college), induction days, Black History month, creative arts weeks, and student awards. There is a news section highlighting current news such as the Student Award Ceremony and the experience of catering students working at Royal Ascot. The college celebrates learner success in its termly magazine 'MakingWaves.' 'Student soundbites' offer student opinions on the different courses offered. Marketing information also places a strong emphasis on the success of their learners in competitions. All of this information contributes to an impression of the college as a vibrant learning environment.

Information on the qualifications and courses it offers

The learning provider should provide clear and well-structured information on the qualifications it offers. This information should include details of how they are assessed and the supporting administration. The relevant sections of Chapters 5 and 6 identify best practice in these areas.

Key facts and achievements

Learning providers will seek to market themselves by highlighting positive statistics and achievements. A further education college, for example, will provide information such as the percentage pass rates and course completion rates for major subjects and the number and percentage of learners who have gone on to university. They might provide more detailed statistics emphasising the number of students who have gone on to study at elite universities such as Oxford and Cambridge. They will highlight ratings given by national inspectorates and also the accreditations gained from awarding organisations, sector skills councils, enterprise initiatives, disability organisations and a wide range of other organisations.

> **Example**
> *The BEET International School and the provision of good information*

> The website of BEET International School is an example of excellent practice. The BEET International School offers English courses and qualifications to teenage and adult students. As well as information on the courses and qualifications available to international language students, the school explains exactly why it represents a high quality destination for students, explaining the significance of accreditation by the British Council, and membership of English UK and QE (Quality English) which again are strong indicators of quality.
>
> The course price list is clearly set out, together with terms and conditions, including the policy on cancellations. There is a course calculator which guides students through the costs of taking different courses. There is a course calendar stating when courses are running and when the exam dates are for the main qualifications being offered by the school. Information on accommodation and visas is clearly provided, together with the associated costs. The school explains what resources it is able to offer students including its library, computer centre and counselling services.
>
> BEET also gives prospective students a good impression of the cultural and social programmes available to students. It provides film nights, dancing classes and pantomimes as well as sports events and frequent excursions to places of interest across England. To encourage student interaction, BEET also manages a Facebook site which keeps students informed about upcoming events. Visiting the website you are given a strong impression of BEET as not just an excellent learning provider but as the hub of a community where you will both be supported and will have lots of fun.

Other important information
A learning provider should explain how the qualifications they offer fit into the wider qualifications system. This will involve explaining how qualification levels work and how they fit into national accredited qualification frameworks.

Most colleges and universities will provide clear statements outlining policy and action in relation to ethical and environmental issues. In the past, the reputation of a number of universities has suffered because of their association with multinationals involved in unethical practices so increasingly this is becoming an important part of the identity of an organisation. A good learning provider will also outline what contribution they make to the wider community.

The importance of the prospectus
A *prospectus* is a brochure providing information about the learning provider and the qualifications it offers. You should be able to access a prospectus as a PDF online or request a free copy to be sent to you.

The prospectus should provide information on a qualification's structure, content, what units or modules are mandatory and which are optional, how the qualification is going to be assessed, and information about what the qualification leads to. A university prospectus should also provide information on scholarships, accommodation and support services that are available to you. There is typically a university prospectus for undergraduates and a different prospectus for postgraduates. Look out for an 'alternative prospectus' where students write about their experiences providing individual viewpoints.

The importance of the student handbook
Many learning providers provide students with a handbook when they start the course. This is common practice in universities, where each department typically produces their own handbook. The basic content of a *student handbook* includes information on the facilities available, contact information for staff, the structure of the qualifications offered and how they are assessed. Some handbooks are much more comprehensive and provide details on the induction programme, the support available while studying and also information on the local area such as

how to register with a local doctor, the location of the nearest banks, local transport links and where to go for entertainment.

Information on pass rates and destination surveys

A good learning provider will highlight their *pass rates* for qualifications in previous years. They might also conduct destination surveys and publish this information. A *destination survey* is conducted by questionnaire and asks learners who have successfully qualified what they are currently doing. For qualifications such as MBAs (Master in Business Administration) this information is an important indicator of the effectiveness of the qualification and can help you compare competing universities in the marketplace.

Student profiles

A good learning provider will publish a range of learner comments and reviews of the services they offer. It is often more interesting to read what real learners felt about a course than to be presented with marketing prose. However a degree of scepticism is required, as only positive learner accounts will be chosen for marketing material.

The quality of resources and learning environment

The quality of the resources and learning environment is an essential part of your learning experience and is an important consideration in your decision. The best way to make a judgement is to visit the building and ask for a tour. The quality indicators below explain what you should look for.

A good computer centre

A comfortable and well-resourced computer centre is a vital part of any learning environment. You want to be able to check your emails and access the internet. You also need a calm environment where you can conduct research and type up assignments.

The best equipped learning providers offer computer centres with a large number of good-quality computers, supported by their own server allowing stable internet access. In addition, they offer free WiFi access for laptop users and they offer a range of e-learning programmes, which can be used free of charge or can be rented. For example a college or university offering research-based modules should give its learners access to computer software, such as SPSS (Statistical Package for Social Sciences), which allows sophisticated data analysis.

Some learning providers offer no more than a couple of old computers and this shortfall in the quality of the resources provided is often not apparent from the website.

The library
The library is sometimes referred to as a 'learning centre' or 'study centre'. A library should be stocked with current journals, books and magazines. It should provide online resources relevant to your area of study and a photocopier that is easy for students to use and does not charge disproportionate fees. The library should provide adequate space for you to do research and should be a quiet environment in which to work. You should not be charged an excessive amount for membership of the library and a good learning provider will have staff available to help you.

Health and safety
It is a basic requirement to provide clear health and safety information. Walking around a learning provider, you should see clearly marked fire exits, a fire alarm, fire extinguishers and evidence of fire alarm testing. You should always be given a health and safety induction on starting a course.

The classroom
Classrooms or training rooms should be spacious, clean, well-lit and comfortable. When visiting a learning provider ask to be shown the classrooms. Have a look at the technology on offer in the classroom. For example, whereas the use of a conventional overhead projector can be considered a basic requirement, computer-linked electronic whiteboards in the classroom signal that the organisation invests money to facilitate teaching.

Class sizes
The ratio between teachers and learners is really important. Many universities deliver teaching through *lectures* given to hundreds of students, supported by much smaller *seminar* groups perhaps involving ten or less learners, which allow for in-depth discussion. You should

check that you will not be consistently taught in a huge class where you have no meaningful contact time with your teacher. Unfortunately, some learning providers do cut teaching costs by cramming learners into huge classes.

The broader environment
However good the teaching and learning resources, student surveys always emphasise the importance of the following features of a good learning environment.

- There should be a prominent noticeboard to display contact information, timetables, exam information, a map of the school and course developments. Details of social activities and clubs should also be posted.

- The canteen is an important social hub in any setting. Some learning providers only provide a drinks machine, others have restaurants offering healthy food and drink.

- The quality of the toilets always provides a good insight into whether the environment is well maintained. Is there somewhere for learners to hang up their coats and put their bags? Is there easy access to a water dispenser or coffee machine?

- Has an effort been made to brighten the environment? Colourful posters, interesting objects, plants and flowers and the colour of paint on the walls all contribute to the quality of the learning experience.

- A comfortable and spacious student room provides a social hub for students and can be used for student clubs and societies. A good student room provides a TV, DVDs and newspapers, information on the local area and it has a comfortable seating area supporting meetings and might also offer a range of board games and other activities.

- An outdoor space where students can relax, get fresh air and play sports is also important.

Accommodation

A good learning provider will provide housing services. The learning provider may manage a network of private accommodation, including for example, bedrooms in family houses. These rooms are often vetted by the accommodation team. Some learning providers may conduct accommodation searches on your behalf or will recommend approved agencies that can provide this service. At the very least you should expect up-to-date information on the price of rented accommodation in the area.

Larger learning providers may provide their own accommodation. The quality of the rooms in halls of residence is an important consideration when starting university. You need to think carefully about the type of accommodation you want. Are you willing to pay a little extra to have ensuite accommodation or are you happy to share a kitchen and shower facilities with a large number of other students?

Additional services

There are other services a learning provider might offer you. There may be gyms and other sports facilities, prayer rooms, airport transfer services, counselling services and, in large universities, even theatres, cinemas, bars, restaurants, supermarkets, nurseries, post offices and other facilities.

The importance of a visit

Many learning providers organise *taster sessions* or *open days* and they are an excellent way of getting to know a place quite quickly. Taster sessions allow you to attend a lesson, lecture or workshop. On an open day you can visit and look around the facilities. You may be shown round by a guide who will give you further information about what the place is like.

Details of open days will be available on the website of a learning provider. You can find details of open days at universities and other institutes of higher education through UCAS. *Opendays.com* also provides a directory of open days covering both universities and also sixth form and further education colleges.

Many areas and regions in the UK conduct *higher education fairs*. These provide an opportunity for you to visit different stalls, collect prospectuses and talk to people from a range of learning providers.

The quality of teaching and support provided by a learning provider

You need to make an informed judgement about the quality of teaching and support provided by a learning provider. However good a qualification is, if it is taught poorly you will not gain the full benefit. You can judge the effectiveness of teaching in the following areas.

The quality of teaching

How well are you being taught in the classroom, lecture theatre or workshop? This depends on the knowledge, competence and professionalism of your teacher. A teacher can be inspirational to listen to, but it is vital that there is coverage of the required content. Chapter 10 outlines what to do if you have concerns over the quality of teaching.

The quality of support

How well are you supported in and out of the classroom? At many universities you have a right to a particular level of academic supervision, often defined in hours of support per academic year. This is your chance to talk through assignment feedback and get advice on how to improve your work.

A good learning provider will also have an effective system of pastoral support. The term *'pastoral support'* refers to support in dealing with non-academic issues. It can encompass managing personal problems, administrative issues, complaints and questions about your future. You have a right to expect this type of support.

Many learning providers ensure learners have their own representatives who can feed back their issues and concerns to teachers and management. Many universities operate *Student Staff Liaison Committees (SSLCs)*, which ensure learner feedback is provided on all aspects of a particular course. These channels of feedback are not just important in terms of dealing with day-to-day issues but also provide an insight into the ethos of the learning provider. A good learning provider will listen and act on the views of their learners.

> **Example**
> *The London Empire Academy working in partnership with students*
>
> Students can provide a rich source of information. The London Empire Academy recently conducted an innovative workshop where it asked over 150 higher education students to form groups and imagine they were the managing director of the college with a small budget for the next financial year. What improvements would they make? The outputs were both creative and cost-effective. Most groups wanted to improve core services such as the computer centre, library and canteen and introduce new technologies into the classroom.
>
> Some recommendations focused on innovation in teaching including student-led teaching seminars to develop presentation skills, using quizzes and debates in a particular subject, using guest lecturers to provide variety, and creating a network of student leaders who could further support student learning.
>
> Proposals to strengthen the student community included reinvigorating the college's social programme through tours and sports clubs, forming a student magazine, and organising a monthly talent show celebrating the different abilities of students. What was noticeable was how engaged students were with improving the college. It was clear that the college played a major role in their lives.

Assessment preparation

How well are you being prepared for assessments? You need to be prepared effectively through revision activities, practice exams, advice on exam technique and by being given a good understanding of the assessment criteria and marking scheme. The quality of assessment feedback is also important. Your teacher needs to provide you with feedback that has sufficient depth and clearly links to the assessment criteria. Feedback needs to allow you sufficient time to review your approach.

Safeguarding the quality of teaching

A good learning provider will take measures to ensure the quality of their teaching. Heads of department and senior teachers should ensure teaching is of a high quality through meetings, monitoring teaching plans and formal observations. Staff should be trained in new teaching approaches and developments in their subject, as part of an ongoing commitment to professional development. A high quality learning provider will often manage a programme of peer observations in which teachers review each other and provide constructive feedback.

As a learner you should be given the opportunity to feedback on the quality of teaching. This should in the first instance be through dialogue with your teacher. However, you should also be given an opportunity to express your views through feedback sessions and questionnaires, both during and at the end of a course.

The quality of service provided to disabled learners

In Chapter 2 we defined 'reasonable adjustments' as the measures that are taken to enable a learner with a disability to participate fully in a qualification. The quality indicators below highlight what you should expect from a good learner provider in this area.

Effective planning

It is not enough for learning providers to make reasonable adjustments on a case-by-case basis. Learning providers have to plan for how they will manage learners with disabilities. This planning needs to inform the design of qualifications, the assessment, and the nature of the learning environment.

Learning providers such as schools, colleges and universities are required to publish an equalities scheme and related action plan. The plan should demonstrate how provision is being improved by taking into account the needs and views of disabled learners.

The adjustments that should be made to support disabled learners

The learning provider needs to ensure reasonable adjustments are made in a number of areas. Learners have a right to participate in a qualification however that qualification is taught, whether it be through lectures, seminars, workshops, laboratories, e-learning activities, fieldtrips or work placements. Adjustments also need to be made to assess disabled learners fairly without undermining the standard of the qualification.

Appropriate adjustments need to be made to ensure disabled learners can access any induction or enrolment activity, careers advice and other support services. It is not acceptable for the physical environment to provide unnecessary barriers to disabled learners. Adjustments need to be made which enable learners to move around the building and use facilities such as the canteen, gym, prayer rooms, library and computer centre. Adjustments also need to ensure learners can gain access to all the resources and equipment which support learning. This could include e-learning packages and the tools and equipment used in workshops and laboratories.

People to speak to
Large learning providers should have a disability adviser, who provides a central point of contact offering advice and support to disabled learners and who keeps abreast with changes in legislation and developments in technology and approach. While this type of designated role might not be possible in a small private learning provider, a member of staff should still be properly trained to provide advice and support where needed. All staff should receive the necessary training in managing the particular requirements of disabled learners.

Transparent information
All policies and procedures supporting disabled learners should be published and readily available. Learners should be able to quickly establish what reasonable adjustments can be made by looking on the website and talking to admissions tutors and disability advisers. Learners should be given clear information on their entitlements to funding such as the Disabled Student Allowance.

Support
Learners should be given the opportunity to disclose their particular disability or special requirement during the application process. In reviewing an application, the learning provider should always work towards enabling that learner to access the qualification.

The different standards for private learning providers
The quality indicators we are talking about here are enforced by legislation passed during the last two decades, including the Equalities Act of 2010. However, it should be noted that these requirements only apply in full to public bodies such as schools, colleges and universities that receive government funding. Private learning providers do not need to meet the same requirements.

> **Case study**
> *Katie reviewing the quality of provision for wheelchair users*
>
> Katie is a wheelchair user. She is applying to her local FE college to study a Level 3 NVQ in Catering and wants to be confident that her disability will not undermine her chance of success. She visits the college website and is reassured to find the college have a published equalities scheme and action plan describing their commitments to supporting learners with disabilities. She contacts the college and speaks to their disability adviser. He reassures her that all the facilities have been designed to allow wheelchair access. He also talks through her anxieties about being unable to fully access the qualification. She is reassured that reasonable adjustments have been made to ensure access to all kitchen equipment and that work placements are vetted to ensure they do likewise.

Customer services and the management of complaints
In dealing with a learning provider you have the right to expect a high level of customer service. You are likely to have numerous questions as you progress through your qualification and you need to know who to speak to. If your question cannot be answered straight away you need to know when you will get a response. In exceptional circumstances you might want to make a complaint. You need to know that your complaint will be effectively managed. The following are indicators of high-quality customer service.

How helpful are the people you speak to?
You should feel relaxed and confident when making an enquiry or raising an issue. People you speak to should give good levels of customer service and should not make you feel defensive or uncomfortable.

The quality of support staff

The support staff or customer services team at a learning provider play a major role in the quality of your learning experience. They should be well trained, courteous and sensitive to your needs, have the necessary knowledge to provide answers quickly and be efficient in coordinating responses to more complex questions. You should always be able to speak to someone and not just communicate via email.

Transparent policies and clear information

There should be a published commitment, often described as a *customer charter*, as to how long it will take the organisation to get back to you in the first instance, and then resolve the issue. Information on who to speak to if you have a question should also be outlined in the induction and in the student handbook.

A good learning provider will try and pre-empt questions you might have by providing regular updates on their noticeboards, website pages or through their teachers. They will also have a well-defined *complaints procedure* available online and in hardcopy form

The management of poor practice

In the qualifications world a distinction is sometimes made between malpractice and maladministration. *Malpractice* is defined as a deliberate act of wrongdoing and *maladministration* is defined as an act of negligence. A good learning provider will have published policies and procedures in dealing with malpractice and maladministration.

If something does go wrong you need to know that your learning provider will act quickly, effectively and consistently. Here are some examples of poor practice:

- A teacher has been unfairly helping particular learners write their assessments. At the extreme there have been isolated cases of teachers accepting money to write assignments for students. This should be acted upon severely.

- Learner data is inaccurately inputted into a computer system causing confusion in the issuing of results. While this is unlikely to be deliberate, the consequences can be serious, so swift and proportionate action is required.

- An assessor is marking papers in an unprofessional and inaccurate manner, this needs to be dealt with immediately by the learning provider as again the consequences are potentially very damaging to the learners involved.

Thankfully these types of incidents are uncommon and you are much more likely to experience high levels of professionalism. The examples relate especially to qualifications. In addition all learning providers should have clearly defined policies dealing and procedures for dealing with bullying, abuse or harassment.

The security of your data
Data management is particularly important in the qualifications arena where organisations have to deal with complex results information relating to thousands of different learners.

You need to know that your personal information will not be used inappropriately and that there is no chance of your results being confused with those of other candidates. A learning provider should manage and track learner data using a robust computer-based content management system. This system should always be protected by security software and require password access. Physical files and the evidence produced for assessments should be organised and stored securely and kept for an appropriate period of time. A learning provider should conduct periodic reviews of their data management and ensure compliance with legislation such as the Data Protection Act.

A robust referencing system should be used to identify you as a unique learner, to register your personal information and to track and manage your results. They should also have contingency plans and back-up systems in case of a serious breach of security, virus or act of nature such as flood or fire. A good learning provider will ensure their staff are properly trained in managing learner data and results information. This training is vital in ensuring that staff input data accurately and are also competent at using the computer-based content management system.

> **Example**
> *The Unique Learner Number (ULN)*
>
> The *Unique Learner Number (ULN)* is the most up-to-date system used in England, Wales and Northern Ireland to manage your data as a learner. The ULN is a government initiative which is designed to replace previous learner registration schemes. The long term aim of the government is for the ULN to be a learner's equivalent to a National Insurance number. It will be a number you take with you, wherever you go and will last you a lifetime. It is designed to be the central reference for all the learning you do, to be used by all the different learning providers you experience. It should be noted that the scheme is still in its infancy and currently coexists with other credible learner registration schemes.

How to utilise inspection reports and other sources of information on the quality of learning providers

This section describes the wealth of information available on learning providers in the UK, including key statistics, inspection reports, the results of national surveys, and consumer reviews.

The value of inspection reports

The various inspectorates working in the UK are described in Annex 4. Here we use the Office for Standards in Education, Children's Services and Skills (Ofsted) and the Quality Assurance Agency (QAA) as examples.

Ofsted inspects a wide range of organisations in England, including schools, sixth form centres and further education colleges, teacher education colleges, learning managed in the workplace, adult and community learning centres, education and training in prisons, and student referral units. The aim of Ofsted is to improve standards and improve value for money in the services it inspects. The frequency of Ofsted's visits is determined by how well a learning provider did in its previous inspection.

The results of Ofsted's inspections are published in a public report, which includes a judgement on the overall performance of the learning provider as well as judgements on specific areas such as teaching and management. Published reports on Ofsted's website include key findings and suggestions for improvements. The learning provider is reviewed using a four point scale: 1 – Outstanding, 2 – Good, 3 – Satisfactory, 4 – Inadequate

Exhibit 7 A sample of questions Ofsted ask when reviewing learning providers

> ✓ How effectively do teaching, training and assessment support learning and development?
>
> ✓ How effective are the care, guidance and support learners receive in helping them to attain their learning goals?
>
> ✓ How effectively does the provider actively promote equality and diversity, tackle discrimination and narrow the achievement gap?
>
> ✓ How efficiently and effectively does the provider use its available resources to secure value for money?
>
> ✓ How safe do learners feel?
>
> ✓ How well do learners achieve and enjoy their learning?
>
> *Source:* The Ofsted website, 2011

Case study
Kristie reviewing the quality of her local further education college

Kristie is planning to start a two year BTEC in Plumbing at her local further education college. She has heard mixed reports about some of the teaching at the college through friends and relatives. She wants to make up her own mind up on the basis of something more substantial. A good option for Kristie would be to visit the Ofsted website and download the latest Ofsted inspection report. She discovers both the college's overall performance and the particular subject she is interested in were rated good by Ofsted in 2010. This gives Kristie the confidence to go ahead and invest in the qualification.

The Quality Assurance Agency (QAA) also conducts external quality assurance, going into universities and impartially checking the standards of teaching and quality of service being provided to students. The QAA 'Institution reports' can be downloaded from their website and provide an overall judgement on the quality and standards of the organisation, together with features of good practice and recommendations for action.

As with any inspection regime, there is debate about how inspections are conducted across the UK, and about the grading system used. Nevertheless, inspection reports do give you valuable information about the quality of a learning provider.

Consumer feedback

Sites are beginning to appear on the internet that give consumer feedback into the quality of qualifications and learning providers in the UK. There seems to be a greater depth of consumer feedback on higher education qualifications in contrast to vocational and professional qualifications. The case study below describes a consumer-focused search engine covering all types of qualifications.

> **Example**
> *Hotcourses – the value of consumer ratings*
>
> *Hotcourses* is the UK's biggest internet search engine for courses, allowing you to search over one million courses by subject, course type or study mode. What makes Hotcourses particularly valuable to a consumer is the 5 star 'overall student experience' rating that it gives to each course, and the unbiased student reviews provided for these courses. Hotcourses also provides consumer reviews on the quality of learning providers. The number of independent consumer-driven search engines is growing with alternatives such as *Push* and *WhatUni.com* providing a similar service specifically focused on the higher education sector.

Other information on the quality of universities

The reputation of universities, in part, rests on the excellence they demonstrate in research. Universities are periodically given a *Research Assessment Exercise (RAE)* rating by the research funding bodies for

England, Wales, Northern Ireland and Scotland. Many of the most prestigious universities in the UK have been given 'world-leading' research ratings. These ratings have reinforced the gap in reputation between the twenty elite universities belonging to the Russell Group, and the large number of less prestigious universities.

The research rating given to a university should not be taken as a direct indicator of the quality of teaching. While there may be a benefit to being taught by lecturers who are leading researchers in their field, it is also possible that a focus on research might undermine the quality of teaching and support given to learners. A university with a less prestigious reputation in research might provide excellent teaching and a comprehensive support package to students.

The *Unistats* website provides statistics and survey results on universities and their qualifications. Unistats provides information on course completion, student achievement and graduate employment and also provides information on the composition of the student population, including information on the proportion of overseas students, mature students and part-time students. Links are also provided to the latest inspection report by the QAA.

Unistats also provides information taken from the National Student Survey, which is conducted annually to highlight student satisfaction rates on individual courses. This is powerful information and the last survey encompassed the views of 222,000 students across the UK. The website also provides statistics on the percentage of students employed with graduate level jobs six months after leaving university.

Performance tables
Two types of *performance tables* are highlighted here. Each year the government in the UK publishes statistics on learners in schools and colleges. This information encompasses a range of statistics including:

- **Social indicators** For example the number of learners who are eligible for free school meals, who have English as an additional language (EAL) or who have some form of special educational needs (SEN).

- **The average grade achieved** This information is presented by qualification for each school and college and for three categories of learners. Learners are categorised as either 'low attaining', 'middle attaining' or 'high attaining' based on their performance before taking the qualifications in question.

- **Performance points** Qualifications are allocated *performance points* by the education authorities in the UK. Qualifications taken in a school in England, for example, are allocated performance points by calculating the size of the qualification and then multiplying this by a value given to the difficulty of that qualification. It should be noted that the methodology used to determine performance point s has provoked significant debate and will change. The current system was strongly criticised by the Wolf Report into vocational education published in 2011.

This information can be found by visiting the School and College Performance Tables on the Department for Education website which covers England, Wales and Northern Ireland. For similar information for Scotland visit the School Education section of the Scottish government's website.

Major newspapers also produce performance tables and these national rankings have a significant impact on the reputation of schools, colleges and universities. If you type in 'performance tables' and the name of a particular newspaper into an internet search engine, you will get links to the latest performance tables for major qualifications such as GCSEs, A levels and degree programmes. There are debates about the research methodologies used in producing performance tables; but they do provide some useful information for you as a qualifications consumer.

Example
The Guardian newspaper

The Guardian newspaper produces a university guide which is available on The Guardian website. It provides detailed university rankings by subject, using the following performance measures:

- The Guardian Score as a percentage. This is a total score derived from the other performance measures below.
- The percentage of learners satisfied with their course. This is based on the National Student Survey.
- The percentage of learners satisfied with the quality of teaching. This is based on the National Student Survey.
- The percentage of learners satisfied with the quality of assessment feedback they get. This is based on the National Student Survey.
- The student staff ratio.
- The expenditure per student by the university.
- The average (UCAS Tariff) grades on entry.
- A value-added score out of ten. This uses a research methodology that allows the value of the students' grades on achieving entry to a university to be compared on an index to the value of the degree they achieved.
- The percentage of students who enter full-time education or a career six months after graduating.

The rational consumer

Before deciding to take a qualification it is worth going on an open day visit, looking carefully at the learning provider's website and prospectus and reviewing inspection reports, performance tables, consumer reviews and survey results on course search engines. This level of research allows you to make confident and well informed decisions.

Case study
Andrew considering taking a bachelor's degree in Law

Andrew is 35 years old and is contemplating a major career change. Andrew has identified a number of possible universities where he could study a bachelor's degree in Law. Andrew wants to make an informed decision. Andrew finds it hard to chose between the content of the degree offered in the three different universities he has shortlisted. How can Andrew decide on the right university?

In the first instance Andrew should review the quality of the prospectus and website for each university. He could also interrogate the latest performance tables from one of the major national newspapers in the UK to find out how the different law courses are rated. He should attend some open days as this will allow him to develop a 'gut feel' for the institutions. Andrew could visit the QAA website and download the relevant institution reports. Finally, Andrew could visit Unistats, Hotcourses and WhatUni.com websites to assess reviews given by other learners and the results of national surveys.

Quality indicators

A high quality learning provider has the following characteristics.

- ✓ They have clearly defined entry requirements and manage a robust application process.

- ✓ They provide clear information on their qualifications, resources, student services and extra-curricular activities through their website, prospectus and student handbook.

- ✓ They provide clear evidence of student achievement and student feedback.

- ✓ They have a comfortable computer centre sufficient for student numbers, a well-resourced library and a clean and comfortable canteen and student room.

- ✓ If relevant, they offer a range of high quality support services in areas such as accommodation and student welfare.

- ✓ They provide classrooms which are clean and comfortable and provide the technology and equipment needed to ensure a high quality learning experience.

- ✓ They operate class sizes which are appropriate to the qualification and do not undermine the support given to individual learners.

- ✓ They provide a high standard of teaching and pastoral support.

- ✓ They provide appropriate resources and support for disabled learners.

- They provide a high standard of customer service.
- They deal effectively with poor practice.
- They manage your personal information securely.

Chapter 8
How to get information and advice

This chapter:

→ Highlights the different search engines available when choosing qualifications

→ Describes other useful sources of information about qualifications and learning providers

→ Identifies where to go for help and advice
- As an adult or young learner
- As a disabled learner
- As an international student

Where to search for the right qualification

There are thousands of different qualifications available for you to choose from, so it can be hard to know where to start. Qualifications are often chosen on the basis of convenience; for example, by seeing what qualifications are available at your local college. Convenience is important, but just as the right product might not be available in your local supermarket, the right qualification might not be at available at your local college.

There are other strategies. National qualification search engines provide a good starting point for a search which will give you the full range of qualifications available in a particular area. They allow you to search for qualifications in different ways, by sector, occupation, qualification name, level and so forth. Some of the major national search engines are identified below. The addresses of the relevant websites are listed in Annex 4.

Directgov

Directgov provides comprehensive information on qualifications. This includes details of nearly 900,000 courses and qualifications in the UK and enables you to search for qualifications and the organisations delivering those qualifications by postcode. There are also advanced search facilities which allow you to search by type of learning (evening classes for example), type of qualification, duration and start date. The Directgov service also provides excellent information on how the qualification system works, on funding and on other benefits.

Alternative sources of information in Northern Ireland, Scotland and Wales

- **Northern Ireland** *nidirect* is the official government website for Northern Ireland. It uses many of the search facilities of Directgov UK but is customised to meet specific educational requirements in Northern Ireland.

- **Scotland** The SQA website has a comprehensive search engine for qualifications offered in Scotland. SQA advisers are also willing to run searches for qualifications on your behalf and can be contacted through their website. Skills Development Scotland provides the *myworldofwork* website which offers among many services the facility to run detailed course searches.

- **Wales** The *Careers Wales* service allows you to search for over 30,000 courses in schools, colleges, universities and other learning providers in Wales.

The Register of Regulated Qualifications

This website is maintained by the qualification regulators in England, Wales and Northern Ireland. It provides lots of useful information about available qualifications. However, it offers less choice than Directgov as it only lists regulated qualifications. It allows you to search for a wide range of vocational and 14-19 qualifications and supports a search by qualification, unit, sector, level, awarding organisation and occupation. When you select a particular qualification you can click on the title and you reach a page with detailed information on the qualification, including how it is assessed and what the different units cover.

The Universities and Colleges Admissions Service (UCAS)

UCAS provides a directory of higher education qualifications available at universities and colleges across the UK. UCAS provides detailed information on the entry requirements for a qualification, what it can offer you as a learner, access to detailed information on the university or college and links to funding opportunities. UCAS allows you to search through 325 universities and colleges (sometimes called institutes of higher education) offering a range of over 50,000 courses. Around half a million learners use the UCAS service each year.

Prospects

This is the UK's official graduate website. It enables you to search for thousands of graduate jobs and postgraduate courses. It provides career advice and lots of tools supporting career development, offers profiles of universities, describes student life in the UK and has a section designed for international students.

Learndirect service

The *Learndirect service* is the UK's biggest provider of online qualifications and offers nationally recognised qualifications in maths, English, IT and business management. Because Learndirect qualifications are online, you can study their qualifications in your own time and in the comfort of your home.

> **Example**
> *The Learndirect service*
>
> Formed in 2000, to date 2.65 million learners have taken over 7 million courses. Learndirect specialises in offering certificates in adult literacy and numeracy, IT qualifications, a range of NVQs and business related qualifications and other university level qualifications. Learndirect provides its qualifications online but also has a network of centres where learners can go to access the internet. It provides its learners with ongoing support at its centres and by phone and email. Some of the Learndirect qualifications involve *blended learning* which is learning in a number of different ways. For example, it offers a number of university level qualifications that involve both working online, taught modules and distance learning.

Other places to search for learning providers

The organisations above all provide good search engines for learning providers, alternative sources of information are listed below.

- **Your local council website** Your local council provides a hub of useful information about learning providers and other education services in the area.

- **UK Register of Learning Providers** You can go to the UK Register of Learning Providers (UKRLP) website and type in your post code. This will generate a list of the registered learning providers in your locality, including contact information, inspection reports, other performance indicators and samples of qualifications provided by that institution. While the UKRLP is a good source of information it makes no judgement on the quality of the learning provider.

- **Edubase** Provided by the Department of Education, this search engine allows you to search for learning providers across England and Wales. The Department for Education in Northern Ireland runs a similar service through the *Schools +* section of its website as does Skills Development Scotland through its *Nearest Centre* Search.

> **Example**
> *The information provided by Dorsetforyou*
>
> The local councils in Dorset provide a wide range of information on the education and learning services in the area. This includes detailed information on schools and colleges, adult learning courses and libraries. The website service provides specific information for parents on early years provision and childcare support. Information is also available on outdoor education opportunities, extra-curricular activities, such as courses in sport and music, and other forms of training and development available in the area.

Help and advice

You might not be sure what level of qualification to apply for, or even what type of qualification might be the right next step. When you find a qualification that looks appropriate, you might still find that some of the information is unclear. Don't worry! There are people to talk to and excellent sources of information available in all of these scenarios.

Where to go to for help and advice as an adult learner

One option is to talk through your skills or interests with a professional *careers adviser*. They have the knowledge of the qualifications landscape to help you decide on what qualifications might be appropriate. Things to remember when preparing to talk to a careers adviser:

- ✓ It is worth making a note of your work experience and qualifications to date. Having your CV to hand is a good idea.

- ✓ Brainstorm the ideas you have about retraining and discuss them with a professional careers adviser. They are there to listen and to support you.

There are a range of national careers advice services provided across the UK.

- In Northern Ireland you should go to Careers Service Northern Ireland in the *Careers* section of nidirect.

- In Scotland you should go to the myworldofwork website.

- In England if you're an adult learner you should go to the *Next Step* section of Directgov. If you are a young learner between the ages of 13-19 you should go to the *Young People* section of the Directgov website.

- In Wales you should go to Careers Wales service.

The Next Step service is a case in point. The Next Step service provides comprehensive careers advice for adults across the UK. Careers advisers are available to talk through the skills that are needed for a particular job, what courses and qualifications are available, and what the cost implications and funding options might be. This service is linked to the Directgov search engine in providing information on over 900,000 courses. A range of other services are provided including tools helping you to review your values, skills and interests; help with CV writing, interview technique and application writing; and forums in which people have shared their experiences.

> **Case study**
> *Holly wanting to train as an EFL teacher*
>
> Holly is 21 and is interested in teaching English as a foreign language (EFL). A learning adviser would talk through the options, highlight what skills are needed to teach EFL and explain what the potential cost and funding options might be. Holly would also be able to look up a job profile of an EFL teacher which describes what the job is like, what the working conditions might be like, what qualifications and experience an employer would look for and what knowledge and skills she would need to demonstrate. She would also find information on what salary and other benefits she could expect, where she could go for more advice and what opportunities there were in the career field.

Supporting you back into the workplace

There are a range of initiatives designed to support people back into work. These schemes and the funding they attract change over time and are subject to a great deal of political intervention. The most reliable sources of information on current schemes is through government services such as the *Directgov Jobcentre Plus* service. The Jobcentre Plus network helps you find jobs and is responsible for paying benefits to people of working age (i.e. 16 to 65). The Jobcentre Plus advisers provide advice and information about retraining and re-entering the workforce.

Case study
Bill seeking to retrain after redundancy

Bill was recently made redundant. His confidence has taken a knock and he is looking to reskill to get back into work. What are his options and next steps? Bill could use the powerful training search engine powered by Directgov. This would allow him to search for training opportunities by occupation and then region. Bill could also organise a meeting with a Jobcentre Plus adviser who would brief Bill on the government schemes supporting retraining back into work. Bill would also benefit from talking to a careers adviser at the Next Step service.

Literacy and numeracy skills
The UK government's *Skills for Life Survey* was published in 2003. It found that 6.8 million adults had numeracy skills below the functional level and 5.2 million adults had literacy skills below the functional level needed to effectively manage everyday tasks and overcome common problems.

Millions of adults in the UK still struggle with literacy and numeracy skills. The UK government has set the target that 95% of adults will have achieved a basic level of functional literacy and numeracy by 2020. The government set a midpoint of 2.25 million learners improving their skill levels; this target was achieved in 2008.

The Move On service
The Move On service is a national project campaigning for the promotion of skills for life in literacy and numeracy. The website contains lots of information and tools promoting the development of these skills.

The Big Plus website
Managed by *Skills Development Scotland* this service provides a helpline and a range of resources supporting reading, writing and numeracy skills in Scotland.

BBC skillswise website
The *BBC skillswise* website has lots of tools and games promoting literacy and numeracy skills.

> **Case study**
> *Graham seeking to develop his numeracy skills*
>
> Graham is a father of two. His eldest daughter is 10. His daughter is bringing back increasingly demanding homework, particularly in maths. Graham lacks confidence in numeracy and is keen to develop his skills. He is considering spending some money on a qualification, if he can find one that suits his needs. What are his options?
>
> It is possible that the qualification could be free of charge if Graham meets certain eligibility requirements. He can also use the Move On website to locate test centres for National Certificates of Numeracy, which are part of the national suite of Skills for Life qualifications. Graham could take the mini numeracy test available on the Move On website to establish his current level. The Move On website provides a range of online training resources to help him prepare for the test.
>
> If Graham wanted to do a nationally recognised qualification which was flexible around his job and his role as a parent, then one option would be to visit the Learndirect website. Graham could study at a time convenient to him through one of the many online courses on offer.

It is easy to rush the purchase of a qualification and not ask for help and advice. Luckily, in the UK there are good sources of information which not only explain how different qualifications might benefit you but also provide more general careers advice and help you research the financial implications of any decision you make.

The key for you as a rational consumer is not to be afraid to ask.

Where to go to get help and advice as an international student

The British Council provides an excellent starting point for students wanting to study in the UK. Through its *educationuk* website (available through its main website) it provides detailed information on all aspects of UK life and culture. Candid information is provided about the challenges and opportunities the UK will present to an international student. This information is highly practical and includes advice on visas, student discounts, contacting home while in the UK, details on how to find accommodation and travelling across the UK. The website has an excellent section of advice on applications and entry requirements for UK learning providers and provides a search engine for UK qualifications. The British Council also provides a *prepareforsuccess* learning hub that supplies a range of activities designed to develop the skills needed to study in the UK.

There are other good sources of information available. The UK Council for International Student Affairs (UKCISA) website has a section devoted to international students studying in the UK. The *GostudyUK* website provides an informal source of information and advice. It provides information on courses, what it is like to live and study in the UK, a helpful glossary of terms and student forums. If an international student wants to make a broad equivalency between the value of their qualification and UK qualifications, the most authoritative organisation is UK NARIC. More information on UK NARIC is available in Chapter 9.

Where to get help and advice as a disabled learner

There are a wide range of organisations who can provide help and advice on funding and your rights as a disabled learner. Some of these organisations are listed below. A national charity providing resources and support relating to your specific disability would also be a good source of information.

- Directgov UK provides lots of useful information about rights and funding for disabled learners and represents a good starting point in any further search for information.

- The national careers services across the UK, which are listed earlier in the chapter, all have sections on your rights as a disabled learner.

- Larger learning providers, such as schools, colleges and universities are likely to have a disability adviser who you can talk to about the management of your disability.

- The Skills Section of the *Disability Alliance* website. Disability Alliance is a national charity which has a specific section supporting disabled learners. The Disability Alliance website provides online resources, factsheets for disabled learners and a free helpline service.

- *AbilityNet* is a UK charity providing support on the use of technology for disabled adults and children.

- *Capability Scotland* is the largest disability organisation in Scotland and can provide general advice to disabled learners.

- *LEAD Scotland* is an organisation committed to widening access to education and learning for disabled learners.

- *Foundation for People with Learning Disabilities (FPLD)* is an organisation that uses research and projects to promote the rights and opportunities of people with learning disabilities.

Chapter 9
Going abroad with your qualification

This chapter:

→ Explains how qualifications travel across national boundaries

→ Provides some tools you can use to prove the value of your qualification when you are in another country

People are constantly moving across national boundaries to seek new opportunities. As an EU citizen you can work anywhere across the European Union, but this mobility creates challenges and questions for you as a learner. For example:

✓ How would your Level 3 BTEC in Leisure and Tourism be treated in Scotland?

✓ How would your degree in Politics from the University of Toulouse be viewed by employers in England?

✓ How can you establish whether you are qualified to work in a graduate job in Germany?

Traditionally, qualifications have been difficult travellers. Until recently if you were living in England and wanting to move to Scotland, the Republic of Ireland or to another EU member state, there were no formal systems in place supporting the recognition of qualifications between different countries. There was no means of formally proving the value of your qualification for use in a different country.

A formal system of recognition needed an agreement between different countries as to how qualifications could be understood and accepted in those countries. Governments needed to agree how their qualifications compared and needed to gain the support of both employers and learning providers.

However, things have now changed significantly. The first significant development was the creation of a *Qualifications Framework for the European Higher Education Area (EHEA)*. This framework provides a reference system for universities and other institutes of higher education across the 46 countries that make up the EHEA. It allows the value of university degrees to be compared and encourages learners to study across Europe. Schemes such as the Erasmus Programme enable over 200,000 higher education students to study and work abroad each year.

Another important development has been the creation of the *European Qualifications Framework* (EQF). This framework allows all the major groups of qualifications in the UK, for example, to be compared with similar qualifications across the European Union. More information will be provided on the European Qualifications Framework later in the chapter.

This rest of the chapter describes the available tools and systems at your disposal to assert the value of your qualification to employers and admission tutors in a new country.

'Qualifications can cross boundaries'

Qualifications can cross boundaries – a rough guide to comparing qualifications in the UK and Ireland has been developed by the education authorities in the UK and the Republic of Ireland. The guide positions the different qualification frameworks in the UK and the Republic of Ireland next to one another and shows the broad equivalencies between the different framework levels. It also highlights how these qualification frameworks reference to the EQF. The guide is frequently updated, so to get the latest version of the guide enter the title into a search engine. The web-based version of the guide also explains the different levels in each of the qualification frameworks in the UK and Ireland.

Case study
Ayesha travelling from London to Scotland

Ayesha is 19 and is moving from Birmingham to Glasgow for family reasons. She has a Level 3 BTEC in Leisure and Tourism. She wants to apply for assistant management positions within the leisure industry in Glasgow. Ayesha has done some research and has found that Scottish qualifications use a different level system, and that a level 3 in the National Qualifications Framework in England looks more like a level 6 in the 12 level system used in Scotland. Ayesha is anxious that employers will not accept her qualification and that she will be unable to effectively prove its value.

Ayesha should download a copy of the *rough guide*. It will show that her qualification is broadly equivalent (in difficulty) to a level 6 qualification in the Scottish Credit and Qualifications Framework (SCQF). She should take this guide with her to interviews with Scottish employers in Glasgow. The guide has no formal status, in that it does not have to be accepted by the employer or an admissions tutor. However the guide does carry weight because it was produced by the education authorities across the UK and the Republic of Ireland.

UK NARIC
UK NARIC provides official information on how UK qualifications compare to international qualifications in over 180 countries. It is designed for learners who want to make a broad equivalency check between the qualifications they have gained overseas and the qualifications awarded in the UK to establish whether they have the skills and qualifications needed for further study or an occupation in the UK. The UK NARIC is part of an ENIC NARIC network of information centres providing a similar service across the member states of the European Union.

> **Case study**
> *Frédéric, travelling from France to England*

Frédéric is 27 and has worked in local government in France for five years. He has a bachelor's degree in politics from the University of Toulouse. Frédéric has set his sights on working in London, but he is anxious that in applying for government jobs in London he will have no way of demonstrating the value of his degree.

Frédéric could use the UK NARIC service and for a charge, UK NARIC would generate an equivalency which Frédéric could take to prospective employers in London. Frédéric needs to remember that while UK NARIC is recognised as the most authoritative source in providing comparisons between UK and overseas qualifications, the equivalencies generated by its service are not binding for employers or admissions tutors. Nonetheless having the equivalency generated by UK NARIC means that Frédéric can be proactive and make a powerful case in asserting the value of his qualification.

The European Qualifications Framework (EQF)
European Union member states have referenced the levels of their national qualification frameworks against the levels of a *meta framework* called the *European Qualifications Framework (EQF)*. A meta framework

can be described as a skeleton framework which links together real frameworks containing real qualifications. So the EQF will not contain real qualifications itself but allows you to compare the value of qualifications in different countries. The EQF has eight levels and can be described as a translation tool which translates the value of your qualification across the different countries of Europe.

The European Commission's Compare Qualifications Framework's interactive table allows you to map the level of your qualification against other qualification frameworks within the European Union. The address of this website is listed in Annex 4.

An example of the comparisons generated by this table is given in Exhibit 7. In this example the Qualifications and Credit Framework is referenced for England and Northern Ireland to allow for a comparison with Malta. While some of the example qualifications given do not sit in this framework they are at the same level of difficulty.

It should be noted that you can currently only compare a small number of qualification frameworks using this interactive table as the majority of EU member states have yet to map their qualifications frameworks against the EQF. This comparison tool does, however, have the potential to develop into a valuable source of information for learners across Europe.

The levels of the national frameworks in the EQF are defined by their level of difficulty and not by how long a qualification takes or what type of learning provider delivers that qualification. It is important to note that the EQF is not designed to change how individual countries organise their own qualifications.

The really important year in the life of the EQF is 2012. By the end of 2012 the certificate or supporting transcript of every regulated qualification across different countries in the European Union will have to make a link or reference to the European Qualifications Framework. For learners like Ayesha and Frédéric, whose situations were described earlier in this chapter, this matters a great deal. They will be able to use the EQF reference on their qualification certificate or supporting transcript to demonstrate the value of their qualifications when they move abroad. This will provide valuable evidence when talking to an employer or admissions tutor in a different country.

Exhibit 8 An example of how the EQF works

England and Northern Ireland	EQF Levels	Malta
QCF Level 1 GCSEs Grades G - D Foundation diploma (England only) National Vocational Qualifications (NVQ) Level 1 Functional Skills Level 1 (England only) Essential Skills Level 1 (Northern Ireland only)	EQF Level 2	MQF 2 Secondary Education Certificate (SEC) Grade 6-7 in academic subjects offered in compulsory education such as languages, sciences and arts MCAST Foundation Certificate ITS Foundation
Entry Level 3	EQF Level 1	MQF 1 School Leaving Certificate (end of Compulsory Education) Key Competences Certificate (provided by the Employment and Training Corporation) MCAST Introductory Certificate Adult Learning Certificate (provided by the Directorate for Lifelong Learning)

Source: European Commission website – Compare Qualifications Framework

Other useful tools and sources of information

There is a range of other sources of information for people moving abroad. Many private companies offer a support service to professionals relocating abroad and this includes information on education systems and qualifications. Both the living abroad section of the Directgov website and the living abroad section of the Foreign and Commonwealth Office website provide lots of useful information and advice. The UK Council for International Student Affairs (UKCISA) website also provides a hub of resources and contacts for UK students planning to study abroad. This includes advice on visas, the recognition of qualifications abroad, sources of funding, and links to information relating to specific countries.

There is a range of tools and resources you can use if moving between countries within the EU:

- The Education and Youth section of the European Commission's *Your Europe* website provides detailed advice about schools, universities and traineeships by country.

- The website *The European Employment Services (EURES) European Job Mobility Portal* provides information about the working environment and job market in different EU member states. The portal also provides a search engine for learning opportunities in the EU and access to a network of 850 specialist advisers designed to support job seekers moving across the EU. The portal also provides information on learning opportunities in the EU.

- EUROPASS provides a common template for you to present your curriculum vitae and language skills. EUROPASS is designed in a format which is recognised by employers across the EU.

- The Leonardo scheme supports learners on vocational programmes to experience training in another EU country.

- The European Credit, Transfer and Accumulation System (ECTS) supports the transfer of credit from one qualification to another across different countries within the EU. It should be noted that this scheme is still in its infancy.

Case study
Paul moving from Belfast to Berlin

Paul's girlfriend is German and he has decided to move to Frankfurt to live with her. Paul is anxious about how his qualifications and experience working in advertising will be viewed in Germany. He has been learning German for the last three years and has reached a competent level. Paul wants to find out more about the German job market and how his qualifications will be viewed.

Paul could visit the EURES Job Mobility Portal which contains a Living and Working Conditions database that would provide Paul with information on accommodation, the tax system, the cost of living, health, social legislation, and the comparability of different qualifications. *The Labour Market Information* section of the EURES Portal provides information on current trends in the European labour market by country, region and sector. Paul could use this information to start exploring the viability of an advertising career in Germany. This area of the portal also contains an events calendar that he could use to search for upcoming events for jobseekers and employers in Germany.

Finally, Paul could create a CV and document his language skills in the EUROPASS template and ensure that he had referenced his existing qualifications against the European Qualifications Framework. This would increase Paul's chances of gaining recognition in Germany for his qualifications and previous work experience.

A global market for qualifications
Qualifications are increasingly mobile across national boundaries. Qualifications can be recognised by the education authorities in the UK but delivered in a wide range of centres across different countries. The internet further supports the mobility of qualifications across national boundaries. It is now very easy to study a UK-based qualification with a learning provider in Hong Kong, for example.

This global market for qualifications has challenged conventional thinking on both the delivery and quality assurance of qualifications. The education authorities and qualification developers in the UK face logistical difficulties in ensuring the quality and protecting the reputation of their qualifications when they are taught in distant countries.

However, this trend towards globalisation shows no signs of abating as national boundaries become increasingly less significant. Despite the challenges noted above there are great opportunities for the UK industry. The 'UK brand' is powerful in the world of qualifications. Leading qualification developers such as Cambridge, Edexcel, and City and Guilds have become major exporters. There are also rich opportunities for learners both in the UK and abroad. International competition provides ever greater choice. There are increasing opportunities to combine studying with an experience of different cultures and proving the value of your qualifications is becoming less of a barrier to living and working in a different country.

Chapter 10
Your rights as a qualification consumer

This chapter:

- → Explains who is accountable for your qualification

- → Outlines your rights as a qualification consumer

- → Describes common problems you might face in taking a qualification and examines your options in dealing with these problems

Who is accountable for your qualification when something goes wrong?

When you take a qualification you will come into contact with people and organisations with high levels of expertise who are dedicated to providing an excellent customer service. But, as with any service, things can go wrong. This chapter explains what you can do if your qualification is not meeting your expectations, or if a problem arises.

The organisation responsible for resolving your problem will either be the learning provider or the qualification developer. Since the learning provider is your main point of contact you will usually go through them and get their help, even when the problem relates to the qualification developer. In either case, if you are not getting satisfaction your ultimate recourse is the education authorities. The organisation you need to contact depends on the type of qualification you are taking and the type of problem you are facing. Annex 4 outlines the different roles and responsibilities of the education authorities in the UK.

Accountabilities summarised

- ✓ The overall standard of a qualification and, in particular, the quality of the assessment are the responsibility of the qualification developer. Qualification developers are quality-assured by a number of different qualification regulators.

- ✓ The quality of teaching and the resources provided to support that teaching are the responsibility of the learning provider and are subject to reviews by the different inspection bodies. It is important to note that different organisations regulate qualification developers and inspect the quality of teaching in learning providers.

- ✓ Sometimes the same organisation develops and delivers the qualification. This is the norm in higher education where, for example, both the overall quality of the qualification and the quality of the teaching is the responsibility of a university.

These distinctions matter because they determine who you need to speak to if you are having a problem. Is the issue how the qualification is being taught, or is it a more fundamental issue to do with the content of the qualification or how it is being assessed? Initially you will probably talk to the organisation that is teaching the qualification but, as an informed consumer, you need to be clear on accountabilities.

You might feel uncomfortable making a complaint, however you invest considerable time, effort and money into a qualification and it is your right to receive a high quality experience.

Your fundamental rights as a qualification consumer

Your rights in relation to a qualification you are studying are summarised below. These rights underpin all the transactions you make as a qualifications consumer, described in the previous chapters of this book.

- ✓ The right to good customer service.

- ✓ The right to teaching of high quality.

- ✓ The right to a well-resourced and comfortable learning environment.

- ✓ The right not to be discriminated against.

- ✓ The right to be charged a fair price and to be clear on what you are paying for.

- ✓ The right for your qualification to be clearly described and to deliver on its marketing promise and stated purpose.

- ✓ The right to be confident in the standard of your qualification and to know clearly how it compares to other qualifications.

- ✓ The right to reliable and fair assessment practices which produce accurate and timely results .

- ✓ The right to have your work remarked, appeal your results, or resit your examination.

- ✓ The right to complain and for that complaint to be dealt with effectively.

- ✓ The right for your personal information and results to be managed securely.

- ✓ The right to receive a uniquely identifiable qualification certificate within a reasonable timeframe.

Examples of the problems you might face are outlined below with general suggestions about what you can do.

The right to good customer service

Poor customer service can have many consequences, both for you and also for your teachers. You are likely to interact with a range of different people on timetabling, the timing of assessments, accommodation, paying for the qualification, extra curricular activities, and how to deal with any difficulties. Your teachers will depend on good customer service in dealing with certain arrangements on your behalf such as confirming assessment dates and clarifying what additional time might be given to learners with special requirements.

Scenario

You are an international student and are studying for a Level 5 Diploma in Marketing at a private college. Your college has agreed to provide a letter confirming your status as a full-time student enabling you to open up a bank account in the UK. You were told it would take five working days to produce but you have been waiting ten days and have not received the letter. You have made numerous calls to the customer services team and have unsuccessfully tried to contact a more senior manager.

What can you do?

If after trying to resolve the delay informally you have had no success, you should consider referring to the college's published complaints procedure and writing a formal letter of complaint. The first step is to establish clearly how long the complaints process takes, and to whom you should address the complaint. This type of issue should be resolved quickly with no need for further recourse. If you have repeated experiences of poor customer service then you may wish to make a formal complaint to the education authorities. Please see Annex 4 for more information on the organisations you might contact.

Scenario
You are a teacher responsible for a learner with dyslexia taking their GCSE in English. You need to establish the rules for the examination she is about to take and specifically what additional time she might be entitled to. You have phoned the awarding organisation for more information but have not received an adequate reply.

What can you do?
The complaints procedures of the awarding organisation should be clearly described on their website. If, after pursuing a complaint, you still feel the service you have been given is poor you can make a complaint directly to the qualification regulator with oversight for that organisation.

The right to teaching of high quality
You have a right to teaching of high quality that delivers the content outlined in the qualification's marketing material, and which develops the knowledge and skills needed to pass the assessments. Poor teaching undermines your chances of success.

Scenario
You are a first year university student studying towards a BA in Law. Your relationship with your seminar tutor has broken down. You do not think she provides adequate support and guidance and seems uninterested whenever you approach her. You are concerned about your own progress but also want to provide general feedback on the performance of your tutor.

What can you do?
It makes sense in the first instance to try and resolve the situation informally within your department. In many cases speaking directly to your seminar tutor might bring about a positive change. But if this feels uncomfortable, there are a number of people who should be able to help. They include your *personal tutor*, who has a pastoral responsibility for your welfare, and the student course representative who has been

elected to feed back issues relating to the course. You also have the option of speaking to the head of department about your concerns. Options include moving to a different seminar group or taking a different module.

Scenario
You are an adult student attending evening classes at a large further education college. You are working towards your Level 1 Certificate in Adult Literacy and are practising for the national exam. When discussing model answers in preparation for the exam you get a strong sense that your teacher is unclear as to what constitutes a pass mark. You are also frustrated by the fact that your teacher often ends the classes early and seems to lack focus in his teaching.

What can you do?
In the first instance, try and deal with the matter informally with your teacher. If this is not successful you could raise your concerns with the head of the department. Should you still need to take the matter further, the college's complaints procedure outlines your next steps. In the unlikely event you exhaust the college's complaints procedure you can make a formal complaint to the Skills Funding Agency, which retains a regulatory oversight over publicly funded adult qualifications.

The right to a well-resourced and comfortable learning environment

In Chapter 7 we described a high quality learning provider and highlighted the value of visiting a school, college or university. This is the best way of judging the quality of a learning environment before spending your money. However, after enrolling you have continuing rights as a consumer. You have the right to expect the resources and learning environment to reflect the claims made on a website or brochure.

Scenario
You have paid for, and started, a Level 7 Postgraduate Diploma in Business Management in a small private college. On arrival you are very disappointed with the quality of the learning environment. The building's location is very different from the description in the marketing

material. The 'modern computer centre' turns out to be little more than five old computers and the library resources are limited in scope and outdated.

What can you do?
The quality of the learning environment is something you are unlikely to change. However, you have every right to complain, particularly if there is a significant disparity between the marketing promise and the reality. Again, in the first instance you should follow the learning provider's complaints procedure. In particular, if you want a refund or partial refund of your fee, this will have to be negotiated with the management through their complaints procedure. In practice, the learning provider's cancellation policies may make it very difficult to gain a refund.

If you feel seriously aggrieved you have some other options. You can make a formal complaint to the awarding organisation responsible for the Level 7 Postgraduate Diploma in Business Management. It might also be worth writing to the trading standards officer with jurisdiction over trading standards in that area.

The right not to be discriminated against

As a learner you have the right not to be discriminated against both in the teaching and assessment of your qualification. Your rights are enforced by a government legislation which covers discrimination on the basis of gender, sexuality and sexual reassignment, race, marital status, pregnancy, religious belief and age. If a qualification uses content which causes you offence on any of those grounds then you also have the right to complain. Discrimination is defined by your perception of what is unacceptable, so if you are made to feel uncomfortable that is a legitimate ground for complaint.

As described in Chapters 6 and 7 if you have special requirements you have the right for reasonable adjustments to be made enable you to access a qualification. These rights are enforced by the Disability Discrimination Act of 1995 and the Disability and Equality Act of 2010.

Scenario

You are hearing-impaired and have started your first year at university. In selecting your university you reviewed the university's disability statement and spoke to the disability adviser. You were reassured that, where needed, a sign language interpreter would be provided. However, by the end of your first term, you are disappointed with the level of support you have received. Your interpreter has been unavailable for a number of lectures, and you feel your learning experience has been undermined at times.

What can you do?

In the first instance, you should sit down with the university's disability adviser and clarify your needs and expectations for the next academic term. If the level of service remains unsatisfactory it is worth making a formal complaint through the university's internal complaints procedure. There are also other sources of help and advice. For example, the Directgov service and the Disability Alliance both provide a range of resources and links to confidential helplines.

The right to be charged a fair price and to be clear on what you are paying for

Chapter 4 showed how to evaluate the cost of a qualification and recommended that if the cost information is vague, you should either avoid the qualification or find out more. You have a right to transparent information on the cost of your qualification.

Scenario

You have paid the course fees for a Certificate in Hair and Beauty on the assumption that this represented the full cost of the qualification. However, once embarked on the qualification, you are presented with additional examination costs for each unit of the qualification. On closer scrutiny you do find this information on the website of the learning provider. But the information was difficult to find and you feel strongly that the cost of the qualification was presented in a misleading way.

What can you do?

While you will have to pay the examination fees in order to continue with the qualification, you have every right to complain to the learning provider about how they present the cost of their qualifications. This type of feedback is best given to the senior management team through their internal complaints procedure. If you feel the information was deliberately misleading you should also contact the awarding organisation responsible for the assessment of the qualification who approved the learning provider to offer their qualification. It is their examination costs that are being presented misleadingly.

If you are still dissatisfied you could contact the qualifications regulator. *Economic regulation* has become a key area of activity for qualification regulators in recent years and they have important powers to act in this area.

Scenario
You are the headteacher of a small comprehensive school and the awarding organisation whose French GCSEs you currently teach has just announced a significant price increase for the summer exam. You feel strongly that insufficient notice has been given by the awarding organisation, as you have already agreed your financial plan for the next academic year.

What can you do?
While you are unlikely to be able to influence the national pricing strategy of the awarding organisation, you have every right to complain. You should contact the support team for the qualification in question and highlight your concerns. You can also make a formal complaint through their complaints procedure. Another option is to contact the relevant qualifications regulator to make a complaint. Awarding organisations have guidelines on the notice period for fee increases and the regulator has the power to act if these guidelines are not followed.

The right for your qualification to be clearly described and to deliver on its marketing promise and stated purpose

In selecting a qualification you are often reliant on a qualification description in a brochure or website. As with any product or service you have the right for the qualification you have selected to deliver on its marketing promise. The more time you spend investigating a qualification before spending your money, the less likely you will be disappointed. If information is unclear, pick up the phone and contact the learning provider to find out more.

Scenario
You are an international student and have paid a lot of money for a 9-month preparation course for the IELTS (International English Language Testing System) examination at a small language school. It quickly becomes clear to you that the IELTS course is poorly resourced and poorly structured. You have not been given a syllabus and the lessons are not focused on teaching you the skills you need to pass the IELTS examination.

What can you do?
The first step is to voice your concerns to your English teacher. If, nothing changes, you should then speak to the director of studies in the language school or the student welfare officer. If these discussions do not result in change you could then make a complaint through the school's complaints procedure. Your options might well be limited to being able to claim a refund or part refund because of the terms of the school's cancellation policy.

If, in the end, the language school does not respond effectively to your complaint you have the option of contacting the relevant education authority. In this case, that would be the organisation responsible for accrediting the language school, which is the British Council.

Scenario
The marketing literature supporting a Diploma in Acting and Dance, which is unregulated, is making bold claims about giving you the skills and contacts to succeed in the industry. Having started the qualification you realise this was an exaggeration. In reality, the course provides a poor quality of training and is poorly resourced. The learning provider clearly does not have the promised contacts in the industry. On further investigation you also find out that the course gives the impression of being nationally recognised at level 3 in a national qualifications framework but is actually not. After a number of sessions of the course you ask for your money back, but the learning provider refuses to give you a refund.

What can you do?
You have every right to try and get your money back as this represents a clear case of false marketing. After exhausting the dialogue with the learning provider, you have a number of options. As the qualification is unregulated, the qualifications regulator will have less scope to act. However, it is still worth contacting the relevant regulator and notifying them of the false claims being made. As they have a general duty to protect all learners taking qualifications, they would also take an interest in any organisation which falsely claimed to be nationally recognised. A further option is to inform your local trading standards officer, highlighting the false claims made by the organisation.

The right to be confident in the standard of your qualification and to know clearly how it compares to other qualifications

You need to be confident of the standard of the qualification you have taken. You also need admissions tutors and potential employers to have a similar level of confidence. Ultimately you cannot control any changes to the perceived or real standard of your qualification. If, for example, you are studying a one-year Postgraduate Certificate in Education (PGCE) at university and there is a suggestion that it has become easier to pass, then this could have a detrimental effect on how the qualification is viewed outside. An unsubstantiated press report on the standard of your qualification can have a similar impact. While you have a general right to be able to trust the standard of your qualification there is little you can practically do in this situation. Your power as a qualification consumer centres on doing adequate research before you select your qualification so that you understand its current reputation in the marketplace.

The right to reliable and fair assessment practices which produce accurate and timely results

Given the cost, time and effort invested in qualifications and the significance your results can have on your future direction, you need to be able to trust that your work is assessed fairly and reliably. Unfortunately while assessment systems in the UK are generally robust, there will always be mistakes and areas of poor practice. If you have any doubts about the quality of assessment practice, do not be afraid to act.

Scenario
You are studying for a master's degree in business finance and marketing and you and a number of your fellow students have strong concerns about how fairly the Module 1 written assignments are being marked. There seem to be significant disparities in the marking of the same assignments across different seminar groups and the justifications provided by tutors for these discrepancies are inadequate.

What can you do?
You have the option of appealing the results given; more information about what this involves is outlined on the next page. If you and fellow students believe that something is fundamentally wrong, speak to the head of department, and the student course representative. If informal dialogue proves ineffective you can make a formal complaint through the university's complaints procedure. Your student union's education and student welfare services should also provide further advice and support.

If you exhaust the complaints procedures of the university you have the ultimate recourse of taking your complaint to the Independent Adjudicator for Higher Education. This organisation is an independent body responsible for managing student complaints and appeals.

Scenario
You are the lead teacher in a small learning provider delivering a Level 2 qualification in Improving the Supply Chain in Manufacturing. You are a highly committed professional, but are concerned by the lack of contact you have had with the awarding organisation responsible for the qualification. You do not feel that your team has been given enough information and training to effectively assess the first set of assignments.

What can you do?
In the first instance you should feed this back informally through your external verifier, who is the person in the awarding organisation responsible for ensuring that your assessment processes are fair and accurate. If these discussions do not improve the situation it would be worth

contacting the *lead verifier* who manages the assessment process for your qualification nationally. You could then escalate the issue through the awarding organisation's complaint procedures. As an ultimate recourse you can take your complaint to the qualification regulator responsible for regulating the awarding organisation.

The right to have your work remarked, appeal your results, or resit your examination

Assessment practice is generally reliable and fair. The UK has strong systems of quality assurance to safeguard your rights to be assessed accurately. However, it is also important to trust your instincts. If you feel that you performed significantly better in an assessment than reflected in your results then in many cases you have the right to request a remark.

Scenario
You are in the second year of a bachelor's degree in archaeology and are dissatisfied with the results you have gained in your end-of-year exams. These results amount to 30% of your final degree and you feel strongly you performed better in your examinations than your results suggest.

What can you do?
You need to establish the appeals process outlined by your university. This process will typically involve a number of stages starting with submitting your work to an *appeals board* possibly comprised of the chair of the *board of examiners* in your subject area and other examiners not involved in the initial marking of your examination. This board will then review your appeal within a defined timeframe. In certain situations, for example if issues of bias are uncovered in reviewing your appeal, your work will remarked and further investigations involving the senior management of the university will take place.

If, in reviewing the appeal, the initial mark is upheld by the university and you remain dissatisfied you have the ultimate recourse of taking your appeal to the Independent Adjudicator for Higher Education.

The right to complain, and for that complaint to be dealt with effectively

All of the scenarios outlined in this chapter refer to understanding and using the complaints procedures offered by a learning provider or qualification developer. What if those complaints procedures are ill-defined? You might have been promised a response to a complaint and nothing has happened, or you are simply unable to contact the appropriate person outlined in the complaints procedure. At the end of this chapter a set of principles outline how to make an effective complaint. In every situation there will be sources or information and advice outside of the organisation you are dealing with. If you are not being taken seriously, get external help and also a second opinion. Annex 4 outlines the different organisations you can go to for support depending on the nature of your complaint and the type of qualification you are taking.

The right for your personal information and results to be managed securely

Learning providers and qualification developers are subject to the Data Protection Act 1998. They need to meet legal requirements in ensuring your personal data and results information are kept securely.

Scenario

The results information for you and your *cohort* studying towards a Level 5 Diploma in Environmental Sciences have been lost when the awarding organisation's computer system crashed. The awarding organisation did not have an effective backup system in place and reformulating the results manually is likely to significantly to delay the issuing of certificates.

What can you do?

This represents unacceptable practice and your college, representing your interests, has every right to complain to the awarding organisation. In the short term, the awarding organisation will need to commit additional resources to manually reproduce the results to prevent further delays in the issuing of your certificates. Depending on the severity of the situation, and particularly if it becomes clear that the awarding organisation did not have effective back up systems in place, the college could make a formal complaint to the qualification's regulator with oversight of that awarding organisation.

The right to receive a uniquely identifiable qualification certificate within a reasonable timeframe

Your qualification certificate is an important document. It provides evidence that you have achieved the qualification at a particular grade or level and should be a source of personal pride. Many employers or admissions tutors insist on seeing an original certificate before offering employment or entry onto a course. Because of its value, your certificate needs to be accurate, uniquely identifiable and produced quickly on achievement of the qualification. An organisation that fails to deliver this can be the source of delay and frustration.

Scenario
Your qualification certificate for your NVQ in Travel and Tourism has still not been sent to you. You completed the qualification over three months ago and are in the process of applying for jobs. One potential employer has asked you to provide an original of your certificate and you feel it reflects poorly on you that you have been unable to provide this.

What can you do?
Your first step is to check what timeframe the awarding organisation has committed to in sending you your qualifications certificates. This information should be available in their internal policies and procedures on their website. If it is clear that the awarding organisation is falling significantly behind their own schedules then you should contact customer services and insist on a quick resolution. If this approach proves ineffective you then need to make a formal complaint which outlines the impact of the delay on your job applications.

If you feel the level of service has been unacceptable you might also consider notifying the relevant qualifications regulator responsible for regulating the awarding organisation. Please note in this scenario it might well be the learning provider who represents your interests in corresponding with the awarding organisation.

Scenario

You have recently moved house and in the confusion have lost your Certificate for Teaching English as a Foreign Language (CELTA). You have applied to teach in China and the language school in China is insisting on viewing an original certificate. The awarding organisation is refusing to send you a replacement certificate as a matter of policy and will only provide a certifying statement of results. Furthermore you feel you are being charged an excessive amount of money for this service.

What can you do?

Many organisations refuse to provide replacement certificates, because of the costs involved and genuine concerns about the dangers of undermining the authenticity of original certificates. This creates real problems as a qualifications consumer. In this situation you are going to have to accept the policy of the organisation and do your best to persuade the school that the certifying statement of results represents an authentic record of your achievements.

However, while as an individual you might not be to gain a replacement certificate, it is worth formally complaining to the organisation about the inconvenience their policy has caused you.

The rational consumer

In pursuing a complaint or in seeking to resolve an issue it is worth remembering the following principles.

Preparing your complaint

Make sure you are clear on how the qualification developer or learning provider has marketed itself as your complaint needs to effectively reference what promises have been made to you as a customer. You also need to be clear on what promises have been made to you in terms of resolving your complaint. What timescales have they committed to for giving you a response?

Read the small print. Ensure that you have familiarised yourself with the necessary detail relating to the subject of your complaint. Often, the terms and conditions relating to a service are positioned discreetly at the bottom of a page. You need to be clear about what this information is stating. For example, if you are seeking a full or partial refund make sure you have thoroughly read the cancellation policy.

Familiarise yourself with their internal complaints procedure. How quickly will an initial response be provided? What form will this response take – will it be by email, telephone or in a formal letter? What escalation points are outlined in the complaints procedure? If you are still dissatisfied, who do you speak to next? What options do you have if you exhaust their internal complaints procedures?

The importance of evidence
Accumulate as much proof as you can of poor practice. Clearly log all the actions you have taken in the pursuit of a complaint and keep copies of emails and letters and make notes of telephone conversations you have had with the organisation in question.

Get help and advice
There is a great deal of support and advice. A good learning provider will have impartial staff available for you to talk to. At a university, for example, both your personal tutor and the student union should be able to provide you with support in making a complaint.

It is worth investigating what other organisations can help you at an early stage in your complaint. Knowing the name and role of the regulator or inspectorate with oversight over the organisation in question has a number of benefits. These organisations will clearly outline your rights as a consumer which will help to clarify your thinking.

Referring to your rights as stated by the qualifications regulator also strengthens your position in any negotiations. Go to Annex 4 for a list of organisations that provide a second opinion, practical help and in some cases will investigate your complaint if other options are exhausted.

Take calm and decisive action
Make the complaint as soon as possible. It is important to remain calm and objective in making a complaint. An initial step to resolve a complaint would be informally through face-to-face discussion. This may not always be possible but is an appropriate starting point.

Act like a rational consumer in selecting and undertaking qualifications. It is easy to feel inadequate and perceptions on whether you are getting value for money can be mixed up with anxieties about whether you are good enough to do the qualification. At the end of the day you are paying to get a high-quality service and you have every right to fight for this service.

Annex 1
The qualification frameworks in the UK

The level of your qualification provides important information. It defines the level of difficulty and what the qualification will lead to. The qualification level is used by admissions tutors, for example, to establish whether you have the right level of knowledge and skills to start a course at university.

There are a number of major qualification frameworks in the UK. The scope of these different frameworks is outlined below.

Exhibit 9 The qualification frameworks in the UK

Scottish Credit and Qualifications Framework (SCQF)
Scope: Scotland
This framework encompasses all the main qualification types offered in Scotland including 14-19 qualifications, vocational qualifications and university qualifications. This framework differs from the other frameworks in the UK in that it is composed of 12 levels rather than 9. All the qualifications in the SCQF are given a level and credit allocation.
Examples of qualifications   Access qualifications, Highers, Advanced Highers, Bachelors Degrees with Honours, Scottish Vocational Qualifications.
Framework for Higher Education Qualifications (FHEQ)
Scope: England, Wales and Northern Ireland
This framework contains all the higher education qualifications offered at universities and other higher education institutions.
Examples of qualifications   Doctoral Degrees, Masters Degrees, Bachelors Degrees with Honours, Foundation Degrees, Higher National Certificates (HNC).

Qualifications and Credit Framework (QCF) and National Qualifications Framework (NQF)

Scope: England, Wales and Northern Ireland

These two frameworks cover all those accredited qualifications, outside of higher education, offered in England, Northern Ireland and Wales. The QCF contains credit based vocational qualifications while the NQF contains 14-19 qualifications and other types of vocational qualifications. While these two frameworks include accredited qualifications offered in Wales, the CQFW should be referred to for a complete overview of provision in Wales.

Examples of qualifications
National Vocational Qualifications (NVQ), Higher National Diplomas (HND), Higher National Certificates (HNC), A levels, Essential Skills Qualifications NI, GCSEs, English for Speakers of Other Languages (ESOL).

Credit and Qualifications Framework for Wales (CQFW)

Scope: Wales

A non-regulated qualifications framework which encompasses many types of qualifications offered in Wales including higher education qualifications, 14-19 qualifications and many vocational qualifications.

Examples of qualifications
Doctoral Degrees, Bachelors Degrees, Foundation Degrees, Essential Skills Wales, Welsh Baccalaureate.

The significance of the different qualification 'levels'

The table below highlights the significance of the different qualification levels, in terms of the skills they develop and what they lead to. There are three qualification frameworks in England: the Qualifications and Credit Framework (QCF) and the National Qualifications Framework (NQF) (displayed in the left-hand column) and the Framework for Higher Education Qualifications (FHEQ) (right-hand column). The levels of these frameworks are broadly equivalent in terms of difficulty.

The frameworks are displayed in the shaded rows together with examples of associated qualifications. If qualifications are at the same level this means they are similar in terms of their difficulty, however they might be different in terms of size and content. Information is provided for each level, about the skills you develop and what they can lead to.

Also note that the skills described are generalised and do not reflect precisely the level descriptions in any one of the major frameworks in England.

Exhibit 10 National levels: what they mean in terms of skills and knowledge

The National Qualification Framework (NQF) and the Qualifications and Credit Framework (QCF)	The Framework for Higher Education Qualifications (FHEQ)
Level 8 Level 8 Diploma in Strategic Direction and Leadership	**Level 8 Doctoral level** Doctoral degrees
The skills you develop You are a leader in your field of study. Your expertise and original thinking contribute to extending the boundaries of knowledge or professional practice in your specialist area. You can critically analyse, interpret and evaluate complex information to produce new concepts and theories. *What this level enables you to do* Qualifications at this level are appropriate for leading experts or practitioners in a particular field.	
Level 7 Level 7 Fellowship in Music BTEC Advanced Professional Diplomas, Certificates and Awards NVQs Level 5 Level 7 Diploma in Translation	**Level 7 Masters level** Masters Degrees Integrated Masters Degrees Postgraduate Certificates Postgraduate Diplomas
The skills you develop You have highly developed knowledge of your specialist area, enabling you to develop original solutions to complex problems. You have a thorough understanding of the different methodologies and perspectives informing your subject area. You can design and undertake detailed levels of research. You can critically evaluate the short and long term implications of your work and can lead projects. *What this level enables you to do* Qualifications at this level are appropriate for senior professionals and managers or graduates looking to develop specialist subject knowledge.	

Level 6 National Diploma in Professional Production Skills BTEC Advanced Professional Diplomas, Certificates and Awards	Level 6 Honours level Bachelors Degrees with Honours Bachelors Degrees Graduate Certificates and Diplomas

The skills you develop
You have a specialist, high-level knowledge of an area of work or study. You can use your own ideas to respond to problems and are able to analyse complex information. You are aware of the current developments in your subject area. You can design your own research and conduct detailed evaluations of your own work. You can initiate and lead tasks and processes.

What this level enables you to do
This level is appropriate for learners looking to develop advanced skills in a particular vocational area or area of professional management/practice. It is suitable for learners wanting to gain entry into graduate employment.

Level 5 Higher National Certificates and Higher National Diplomas NVQs Level 4 BTEC Professional Diplomas, Certificates and Awards	Level 5 Intermediate level Diplomas of Higher Education Foundation Degrees Higher National Diplomas

The skills you develop
You have a strong depth of knowledge and skills in an area of work or study and respond effectively to complex problems and situations. You have a high level of work expertise and competence in managing and training others. You can use relevant research and have an understanding of different perspectives in your subject area. You are able to work independently and can take responsibility for courses of action and the work of others.

What this level enables you to do
This level is appropriate for learners wanting to develop specialist skills in a particular professional, vocational or academic area.

Level 4 Higher National Certificates BTEC Professional Diplomas, Certificates and Awards	**Level 4 Certificate level** Certificates of Higher Education Higher National Certificates

The skills you develop
You have strong knowledge and skills in a particular area and can solve reasonably complex problems. You can analyse, evaluate and interpret relevant information and ideas. You have an informed perspective of the different approaches within your subject area. You review the effectiveness of your work and work with a good level of independence. You can take responsibility, where appropriate, for the work of others.

What this level enables you to do
This level is appropriate for learners working in technical and professional jobs, and/or wanting to develop skills in managing and developing others.

Level 3 A levels International Baccalaureate NVQs Level 3 BTEC Diplomas, Certificates and Awards BTEC Nationals OCR Nationals	There is no corresponding level in higher education

The skills you develop
You have the ability to develop a range of knowledge and skills at a detailed level. You can deal with quite complex problems and conduct investigations into your subject. You can use a range of methods in your learning and have an awareness of the different perspectives and approaches within your subject. You can make independent judgements.

What this level enables you to do
This level is appropriate for a qualified or skilled worker or a learner wanting to gain entry into university.

Level 2 GCSEs grades A* - C BTEC Awards and Certificates Functional Skills Level 2 OCR Nationals NVQs Level 2 English for Speakers of Other Languages (ESOL) Level 2	There is no corresponding level in higher education

The skills you develop
You have good knowledge and understanding of a subject. You use this knowledge to complete well defined tasks and deal with straightforward problems. You can interpret and gather relevant information related to a task. You can work independently with some guidance.

What this level enables you to do
This level is appropriate if you are wanting to progress into skilled employment or continue into further education.

Level 1 GCSEs grades D-G Functional Skills Level 1 BTEC Introductory Diplomas and Certificates OCR Nationals English for Speakers of Other Languages (ESOL) Level 1	There is no corresponding level in higher education

The skills you develop
You can use knowledge, skills and procedures to complete well defined tasks. You can select and use relevant information and identify whether actions have been effective. With appropriate guidance you can take responsibility for your learning.

What this level enables you to do
This level is appropriate if learners are wanting to progress in secondary education or to start developing the skills required in a particular vocational area.

Entry level Entry Level Certificates English for Speakers of Other Languages (ESOL)(E1-E3) Functional Skills at entry level (English, maths and ICT)	There is no corresponding level in higher education

The skills you develop
You can use your knowledge or understanding to carry out simple familiar activities with appropriate guidance. This level is divided into three sublevels. As learners progress to Entry 3 they are able to carry out structured tasks and demonstrate an awareness of the consequences of their actions.

What this level enables you to do
This level is appropriate for learners who want to develop core skills enabling them to continue or return to education or training.

Annex 2
An overview of the types of learning provider in the UK

Compulsory education up to 16

The Education Act of 2008 made education compulsory until the age of 18, although this does not come into full effect until 2015. The main phases of compulsory education can be defined as follows. Primary schools across the UK are for 4 to 11 years olds. Primary education is divided into stages – key stage 1 which covers the ages of 5 to 7 and key stage 2, which covers the ages of 7 to 11. In Scotland there is not this subdivision and primary education caters for 5-12 year olds. Secondary education caters for 11 to 16 year olds in England, Wales and Northern Ireland; in Scotland secondary education runs for four compulsory years until the age of 15/16. Some parts of the UK still operate a three tier system involving middle school, for pupils from the ages of 9 to 13. A very small, but growing, number of parents decide to home-school their children.

There are lots of different types of school in the UK. They differ in how they are funded, how they are managed and how they select pupils. Some of them are described below.

Comprehensive schools
Over 90% of pupils in the UK go to schools which are funded by the state. These schools are free to attend. There are many types of comprehensive school – one of the important differences is the relationship between the school and the local authority in relation to setting and managing budgets and recruiting teachers.

Academies
Academies are a type of comprehensive school. An academy has greater independence than a typical state school in both how it spends its money and in what subjects it teaches.

Free schools
These schools have been set up by a voluntary group, such as a group of parents, teachers or a faith group. They are still state-funded but that funding is managed by that voluntary organisation.

Faith schools
These schools promote a particular religion through the ethos of the school and may require learners to subscribe to that religion.

Grammar schools
These schools select all, or most, of their pupils on the basis of academic ability.

Independent or private schools
These schools are funded by private organisations and charge pupils to attend. It should be noted that the term 'private school' is commonly used in the UK qualification system and describes provision for learners of all ages.

Specialist school
A specialist school is given additional funding by the government to focus on specific subjects such as sport or music. Most comprehensive schools in the UK have gained a specialist status in a particular subject area.

Special schools
These schools cater for both young people and adults with special educational needs (SEN).

Pupil referral units
These are schools maintained by the local authority for young people who have been excluded from mainstream schools or who have a condition which prevents them from participating in mainstream education. Exclusions are used by schools to remove disruptive students on either a temporary or permanent basis.

Post-16 education

The post-16 phase of education in the UK encompasses sixth form provision at schools, sixth form centres and also the wider provision offered by further education colleges. The term *further education* is used to describe the qualifications taken by 16 to 19 year olds and adults. The main types of learning provider in this area are listed below.

Sixth form centre/college

A sixth form centre specifically caters for 16-19 year olds and focuses on providing qualifications supporting entry to university. Unlike a further education college, the sixth form centre does not usually provide vocational courses for adult learners.

School sixth forms

School sixth forms generally focus on qualifications supporting entry to university and are typically much smaller than further education colleges. They are connected to a particular school and offer familiarity to learners who have just completed examinations at the age of 16.

Further education colleges

FE colleges cater for 16-19 year olds and adults. The range of qualifications offered can vary depending on what else is offered locally. If most local schools have sixth forms, or there are local sixth form centres, the FE college may specialise in vocational subjects which help develop the skills needed for different jobs. These could include subjects such as plumbing, agriculture or information technology. In areas where the FE college is the only, or main option after 16, they will also offer everything you could get in a school sixth form or sixth form centre.

Higher education and adult learning

Higher education refers to the degrees and other higher level qualifications provided by universities and other higher education institutions. *Adult learning* or *lifelong learning* is provided by a much wider range of learning providers.

Higher education institutions

This is a broad term which includes universities, higher education colleges and other specialist providers who deliver higher level qualifications. In recent years a significant number of colleges (in particular FE colleges) have been approved to deliver courses that lead to degrees awarded by a university. Increasingly you can take a degree at your local college which is then awarded by a university in a different part of the country.

Universities
Universities come under the oversight of the education authorities in the UK and are largely financed through the Higher Education Funding Councils. However they have a strong degree of autonomy. It is up to the management of a particular university to decide what degrees and other qualifications they will offer, and which learners they will accept to study their qualifications.

Employers
Thousands of employers across the UK, often working with awarding organisations, provide an environment in which you can learn the skills and competencies needed to qualify for a profession or further develop your career. Many employers specifically support and sponsor staff taking a relevant qualification. This is often defined as *work-based learning (WBL)*.

Local test centres
There are a variety of local test centres including colleges, Jobcentre Plus centres and even driving test centres in most towns and cities in the UK. These test centres are geared towards the adult learner and provide test facilities for nationally recognised IT, literacy and numeracy qualifications.

Prisons
The prison system across the UK maintains a strong commitment to promoting lifelong learning. There is a strong emphasis on developing literacy, numeracy and IT skills and also developing a range of vocational skills. Prisoners are often able to take a wide range of qualifications in these areas.

Distance and online learning providers
There are many specialist learning providers who provide qualifications through the internet or paper-based correspondence. Typically learning

is conducted through independent study, via the internet or through postal correspondence. Assessed work is often sent to a network of tutors by email or by post. This type of learning is also described as *home study* or *correspondence learning*. The provision of internet based learning in the UK is one of the most dynamic and fast growing sectors of the qualifications industry. These types of qualifications offer the flexibility to study for a qualification in your own time and in the comfort of your own home.

Other private providers
There is a great diversity of private learning providers operating across the UK. For example there are many hundreds of language schools specialising in teaching English as a foreign language to international students. Private providers do not offer qualifications which are publicly funded by the education authorities in the UK.

Annex 3
An overview of the types of qualifications available in the UK

The UK qualifications market can be divided into major groups of qualifications defined by their common characteristics. Some of these are described below.

14-19 qualifications
These qualifications are taken by learners intending to enter into further or higher education or go directly into employment.

A levels
A levels (The Advanced Level General Certificate of Education) are usually taught over two years, the first year at AS (Advanced Subsidiary) level and the second at A2 (Advanced) level. They are graded A* to E. AS levels can be stand-alone qualifications or 50% of a full A level. Learners will usually study 4 AS levels and progress onto 3 A levels. Most learning providers will require learners to have passed 5 GCSEs (A* to C) to begin A-level courses. They are available across England, Wales and Northern Ireland in a wide range of about 80 academic and vocational subjects including Accounting, French, Computer Science and Sociology. They are most suitable for learners wanting to progress into higher education. Most A levels are made up of four units. Assessment is typically by written exam, coursework and, for subjects such as art, an assessment of practical skills.

Cambridge Pre-U
The Cambridge Pre-U is a relatively new qualification for students aged over 16. It is designed to develop the skills needed for university study and fosters the ability to study independently. Subjects can be studied individually, or as a Pre-U Diploma. The Pre–U Diploma consists of three subjects as well as an Independent Research Report and Global Perspectives Course which promotes cross-cultural awareness and an international outlook. Universities accept Pre-Us as equivalent to

A levels. They are available in 27 subjects including Biology, Classical Greek, Comparative Government and Politics, and Music.

GCSEs

General Certificates of Secondary Education (GCSEs) are single subject qualifications. Learners usually study between 8 and 11 GCSEs over the course of two years. They are compulsory for 14-16 year olds in England, Wales and Northern Ireland. GCSEs are available in over 40 academic subjects, and nine applied (work related) subjects at level 1 and 2 in the NQF. Learners in compulsory education are required to study core subjects including English, Science and Maths. At the end of year nine (aged 13-14) learners typically choose which additional subjects they wish to study, in areas such as Art or Modern Foreign Languages. GCSEs are graded A* to G with U as ungraded. In some subjects you are set in a higher or foundation tier which determines the maximum grade you can get. Pass grades (A* to C) in Maths and English GCSEs are commonly required to enter further education and employment.

IGCSEs

The International General Certificates of Secondary Education (IGCSEs) are internationally recognised qualifications devised by the University of Cambridge (with Edexcel offering its own versions). They became popular with British expatriates in private international schools. In similarity to GCSEs, pass grades are A*-C. Over 70 subjects are available, including 30 language courses such as Afrikaans, Arabic and Japanese. As they are designed for an international market, many language IGCSEs are available in two versions, as a first language or a foreign language. They are becoming increasingly popular in private schools and are used to progress onto qualifications such as A levels or Cambridge's Pre-U qualification.

Scottish Highers

Highers (level 6 in the SCQF) are taken by learners in the fifth year of secondary education in Scotland. They are the equivalent of AS levels in England. Learners aged 16-17 usually study five Highers in schools or colleges in Scotland. Highers provide the main route to higher education in Scotland. Highers are graded A, B, C as passes and D and 'No Award' denoting a fail. Highers are available in a wide range of subjects including English, Geography, Latin and Manufacturing.

Advanced Highers are a level 7 qualification in the SQCF. They are designed to give learners an opportunity for in-depth study and independent learning in a specialised subject area. They are required for Scottish learners who want to study in English universities. Advanced Higher courses are the equivalent of the first year of a Scottish university in a particular subject and can be used by learners to enter Scottish universities in the second year (of four) or to enter directly into employment. Learners study three subjects over one year. They are made up of three units which are assessed by teachers in the form of coursework, examinations or practical work and an externally assessed examination or project marked by the SQA. As with Highers, they are graded A, B, C as passes and D and 'No Award' denoting a fail. There are currently 38 Advanced Highers available in subjects such as Administration, Chemistry, Gaelic (Learners) and Product Design.

Standard Grades and National Courses
These are qualifications taken by learners aged 14 to 16 in Scotland in their third and fourth year of secondary education. Learners typically take eight subjects and are assessed by a final exam at the end of their fourth year. Learners are required to study a range of subjects including English, Maths, Physical Education (PE) and Religious, Moral and Philosophical Education (RMPS). Standard Grade exams are tiered at three levels: Foundation level (SCQF level 3), General level (SCQF level 4) and Credit level (SCQF level 5). Learners are marked using a scoring system of 1 to 7.

Standard Grades are being phased out and replaced by national courses and units as part of the Higher Still qualification reforms. Three levels of Access qualifications (Access 1, 2 and 3) have been introduced at SCQF levels 1, 2 and 3. Access level 3 is equivalent to the Foundation level Standard Grade. Intermediate 1 and 2 qualifications have also been introduced which are roughly equivalent to the Standard Grade General level and Credit level respectively. National courses combine units internally assessed by teachers with a final exam marked by SQA.

Welsh Baccalaureate
The Welsh Baccalaureate is available to 14-19 year olds in Welsh schools, colleges and training providers. It is available at three levels: Foundation (NQF level 1), Intermediate (NQF level 2) and Advanced (NQF level 3).

The Welsh Baccalaureate is comprised of two components, a core programme and a set of options. The core programme includes developing key skills and employability skills, conducting an individual investigation, an exploration of issues in modern life and developing an awareness of Wales in both a European and international context. Optional programmes can include qualifications such as GCSEs, A levels, BTECs and NVQs. The core programme is marked pass or fail.

14-19 Diploma
14-19 Diplomas provide learners with the opportunity for practical work-related experience as well as classroom-based learning. They are designed to develop the skills required by employers and universities. There are fourteen diplomas currently available in England, in subjects such as Construction and the Built Environment, Hair and Beauty Studies and Retail Business. Within the context of a particular subject area functional skills are also developed in English, Maths and ICT. Diplomas typically take one to two years to complete, depending on the level and are available at three levels: Foundation (NQF level 1), Higher (NQF level 2) and, for those over 16, Advanced (NQF level 3). 14 -19 Diplomas are marked A* to U, the grading scale varying depending on the level of qualification you take.

Skills-based qualifications

These qualifications develop skills in literacy, numeracy, ICT and language and communication skills.

Core Skills
Core Skills qualifications develop the skills needed in life and work. They are the Scottish equivalent of Key Skills and Functional Skills. Core Skills can be completed automatically with some Standard/Higher qualifications and some SVQs or as stand-alone qualifications within work-based learning or as part of modern apprenticeships. They are available in Communication, Information and Communication Technology, Numeracy, Problem Solving and Working with Others at levels 3 to 6 on the Scottish Credit and Qualifications Framework (SCQF).

Essential Skills Wales and Essential Skills Northern Ireland
ESW (Essential Skills Wales) was introduced in September 2010 to replace the Key Skills and Basic Skills qualifications. It is available in three subjects, Communication, Application of Number and Information Communication Technology. They are suitable for learners wanting to develop the practical skills needed in everyday life, such as reading, writing, numeracy and using a computer. They are available in five levels from entry level to level 4. At entry level assessment is test based and at levels 1 to 4 you are required to produce a portfolio.

Essential Skills Northern Ireland are also designed to develop the skillls needed for everyday situations. They are geared towards adults but are increasingly taken by young people. They are available in Literacy and Numeracy at entry levels 1-3 and Communication and Application of Number at levels 1 and 2. The literacy and numeracy assessments are test based, while the level 1 and 2 qualifications are assessed both by test and a student portfolio.

Functional Skills
Functional Skills are a suite of qualifications designed to replace the Skills for Life and Key Skills qualifications. They are being trialled on a three year scheme in England and are being offered at entry level, level 1 and level 2. They are available in Maths, English and Information Communication Technology to learners aged 14 and over (although younger learners can take them). They are focused on the application of these skills in practical, real life scenarios. Each Functional Skill qualification requires you to pass an end exam. Functional Skills contribute to other qualifications such as Apprenticeships, 14-19 Diplomas and GCSEs.

Key Skills
Key Skills qualifications are designed to help learners improve their abilities in work, education, or at home. There are no entry requirements and they are often studied alongside GCSEs. The main key skills are Communication, Application of Number and Information Communication Technology, with three wider key skills in Working with Others, Improving Own Learning and Performance, and Problem Solving. They are available at NQF levels 1-4 and can be taken by learners at the level most suitable for them in schools, colleges and training providers. At

levels 2, 3 and 4 they can count towards a UCAS application to study at higher education institutions.

Skills for Life
Skills for Life qualifications are usually taken by learners over 16 who have left compulsory education and do not have GCSEs (or equivalent) in Maths, English and ICT. They are for learners wanting to develop skills needed in everyday life, such as reading, writing or maths. Entry level courses consist of tasks which are assessed by teachers. At NQF levels 1 and 2 learners are assessed by 40 multiple choice questions, which can be answered online or on paper. These assessments called National Basic Skills Tests are marked pass or fail and can be taken as many times as a learner wants. These qualifications are suitable for learners who want to boost their confidence in their own skills, improve their CVs, or re-enter education and progress onto programmes such as NVQs. There are courses available in Adult Literacy and Adult Numeracy, ICT (at entry level) and in English for Speakers of Other Languages (ESOL).

Vocational qualifications

These qualifications are designed to develop work-related skills in a particular subject area.

Apprenticeships
Apprenticeships allow learners to train for a particular role while working in that industry. Apprenticeships are frameworks which enable learners to gain a range of nationally recognised qualifications such as NVQs or SVQs, Functional Skills qualifications, Key Skills qualifications or Core Skills, and a variety other knowledge based or technical qualifications. Apprenticeships are offered across the UK, in England alone they are provided by over 100,000 employers in over 200 different areas such as business administration, agriculture and engineering. They typically take between one and four years to complete and are available at three levels: Intermediate Level Apprenticeships (equivalent to five GSCEs), Advanced Level Apprenticeships (equivalent to two A level passes) and Higher Apprenticeships which enable learners to work towards level 4 work-based qualifications. Learners have to be over 16 to entrol on an Apprenticeship.

BTECs

BTECs are available in different levels, from entry level developing the initial skills for everyday life, up to professional development qualifications at NQF levels 4 to 7. They are suitable for learners of a wide range of ages in work-related subjects, with courses available in fields such as Art and Design, Business Studies, IT and Media. BTECs combine the development of practical skills needed for the workplace with the necessary theory in that subject area. The main types of BTEC are graded distinction, merit, pass or some variation of that grading scheme.

Foundation degrees

Foundation degrees are vocational courses which combine work-related learning in a particular subject area with the development of study skills and the general skills needed for work. They are flexible programmes that can be studied part-time, in a work-based environment or through distance learning. Foundation degrees are developed in partnerships between universities, employers and colleges. They are divided into two sectors, Arts (FdA) and Sciences (FdSc). They are available in hundreds of subjects from Environmental Cleaning Management to Offender Management and Sports Therapy. They are suitable for a wide range of learners, who may be wanting to change their career path, develop their career prospects, or enter higher education at a later stage of their life. They can be topped up with additional study to gain a full bachelor's degree. You can be assessed in a wide variety of ways including through project work, practical work and exams.

Higher National Certificates (HNC) and Higher National Diplomas (HND)

HNCs and HNDs give learners the skills required to be effective in a particular field of employment. These qualifications are often accepted towards membership of professional bodies such as the Royal Institution of Chartered Surveyors (RICS). To gain entry onto these courses you usually need to have passed one A level or equivalent. An HNC typically takes one year to complete full-time, while the HND requires two years of full-time study to complete. A completed HNC can enable a learner to progress to the second year of a degree programme while an HND can enable entry to a second or third year of a degree. They are available in a wide range of work-related subject areas including

Agriculture, Construction and Civil Engineering, and Sports and Exercise Sciences. They are marked pass, merit and distinction.

National Vocational Qualifications (NVQs) and Scottish Vocational Qualifications (SVQs)
NVQs develop skills specific to a vocational area through practical, work orientated tasks. NVQs are based on national occupational standards. These standards define what skills are required to do a job competently in a particular industry or sector. NVQs can be taken at work, in college or as part of an apprenticeship. NVQs are available in a wide range of subjects, including Sales, Marketing and Distribution, Construction and Property, and Health and Social care. They are available to young people and adults at levels 1 to 5 (please note that the level 4 NVQ is equivalent to an NQF level 5 and the level 5 NVQ is equivalent to an NQF level 7). Learners are assessed on portfolios and practical assignments by a qualified assessor. That assessor will also observe tasks being performed and will make a judgement on both the knowlege and skills demonstrated by the learner.

Scottish Vocational Qualifications (SVQs) are equivalent to NVQs. There are 5 levels of SVQs, with a wide range of courses available. For more information visit the SQA website.

Postgraduate diplomas and certificates
Postgraduate diplomas and certificates are for graduates who wish to improve their knowledge in either an academic or vocational field. They are available in a wide range of work-orientated fields such as Business Management and Travel, Tourism and Hospitality. They often take between 9-12 months to complete if studied full-time. The method of delivery will vary greatly depending on the subject and learners may be assessed through research projects, coursework or examinations. They are graded at distinction, merit, pass and fail. They can be 'topped up' by further study to become a full master's degree at many higher education institutions.

Bachelors degrees, masters degrees and doctorates
These qualifications develop advanced skills in a particular subject area. Please note that many degrees can be strongly work-related.

Bachelors degrees

Bachelors degrees are commonly divided into two types: Bachelor of Arts (BA) and Bachelor of Sciences (BSc) but there are other variations available, such as a Bachelor of Engineering (BEng). They take three years to complete full-time (or four if they include a year of work experience or studying abroad). They can also be studied part-time, and through distance/flexible learning. Bachelors degrees are graded as First Class Honours, Upper Second Class Honours (2:1), Lower Second Class Honours (2:2) and Third Class Honours. Bachelors degrees are available in an increasingly wide field of subjects, from BA Film Studies, BSc Mechanical Engineering and degrees developing specific skills in an occupation such as BSc Radiotherapy and Oncology. Upon the completion of a bachelor's degree, graduates have the option of entering into graduate level employment or further specialisation in their chosen field through a master's degree or doctorate.

Masters degrees

A master's degree offers a learner the chance to specialise and develop advanced skills in a particular field. Many masters programmes require learners to conduct high levels of independent research. Assessment usually consists of a number of written assignments, reports, presentations and projects as well as an end of year dissertation. A master's degree typically takes 12 months or more to complete, if studied full time. They are often graded at distinction, merit, pass and fail. The types of masters include: Master of Arts (MA), Master of Science (MSc), Master of Business Administration (MBA), Master of Law (LLM) and Master of Research (MRes). Masters degrees enable access to specialised forms of graduate employment or progression onto a doctorate.

Doctorates

Doctorates are an original piece of research undertaken by a learner at a university that has the facilities, expertise and funding required to support research programmes. They typically take a minimum of three years full-time study to complete, although they can take much longer. The first year of a doctorate is focused on planning and conducting the necessary research. The final year of study is normally focused on producing the dissertation to present the principal findings from research undertaken. They are usually graded pass or fail, although it is possible to receive a distinction if the work is viewed as making a substantial contribution to a particular field of study. Doctorates are suitable for learners wishing to develop a highly specialised level of expertise within a particular subject area. Many doctorate programmes, once completed and passed, lead to the qualification Doctor of Philosophy (PhD).

Annex 4
An overview of organisations involved in UK qualifications

If you have a question or issue, in the first instance, you are likely to speak to your learning provider. In this Annex we list some other organisations that can help, with their websites.

Government departments in education

Department for Business Innovation and Skills (BIS)
This department is responsible for promoting skills and developing further and higher education in England.
www.bis.gov.uk

Department for Education
This department is responsible for education and children's services in England.
www.education.gov.uk

Department for Education in Northern Ireland
This department is responsible for administering all aspects of education within Northern Ireland, excluding further and higher education.
www.deni.gov.uk

Department for Education and Learning in Northern Ireland
This department promotes learning and skills for the workplace and is responsible for further and higher education in Northern Ireland.
www.delni.gov.uk

Scottish government
The Scottish government is responsible for all aspects of education and training in Scotland.
www.scotland.gov.uk

Welsh Assembly government
The Welsh Assembly government has responsibility for the development and quality assurance of education and training in Wales (outside of higher education).
www.wales.gov.uk

Qualification regulators and quality assurance agencies

These organisations have the responsibility of quality assuring the awarding organisations that develop and award qualifications and the qualifications.

CCEA (Council for Curriculum Examinations and Assessment)
This organisation ensures the standard of qualifications and examinations offered by awarding bodies in Northern Ireland.
www.rewardinglearning.org.uk

Ofqual (Office of Qualifications and Examinations Regulation)
This organisation is responsible for regulating awarding organisations and the qualifications they develop. This includes 14-19 qualifications and vocational qualifications in England and vocational qualifications in Northern Ireland.
www.ofqual.gov.uk

QAA (Quality Assurance Agency)
This organisation conducts performance reviews of universities and other higher education institutions.
www.qaa.ac.uk

SQA Accreditation
This organisation accredits vocational qualifications offered in Scotland and regulates the awarding bodies which develop those qualifications.
www.sqa.org.uk

Welsh Assembly government
This administration regulates qualifications and awarding organisations in Wales.
www.wales.gov.uk

Inspectorates and accreditation bodies

These organisations inspect the quality of learning providers across the UK including the quality of management, resources and teaching.

Bridge Schools Inspectorate (BSI)
This organisation inspects faith based schools and colleges in England.
www.bridgeschoolsinspectorate.co.uk

British Accreditation Council
This organisation quality assures independent further and higher education in the UK.
www.the-bac.org

British Council Accreditation UK
This organisation quality assures the English Language Teaching (ELT) sector in the UK.
www.britishcouncil.org

Education Scotland
This body conducts inspections of schools, colleges, special schools, the education departments of local education and other organisations.
www.educationscotland.gov.uk

ESTYN
This organisation inspects the quality and standards of education and training providers in Wales including primary, secondary and further education, independent schools, work-based learning and careers companies.
www.estyn.gov.uk

ETINI
This organisation inspects the quality and standards of education and training providers in Northern Ireland including primary, secondary and special schools, further and higher education, the youth and community sector and other organisations.
www.etini.gov.uk

ISI (Independent Schools Inspectorate)
This organisation inspects independent schools in the UK.
www.isi.net

Ofsted (Office for Standards in Education, Children's Services and Skills)
This organisation inspects the quality of schools, sixth form colleges, further education colleges, education and training in prisons, student referral units and other organisations in England.
www.ofsted.gov.uk

School Inspection Service(SIS)
This organisation inspects independent schools and colleges including Montessori and Steiner Colleges.
www.schoolinspectionservice.co.uk

Skills Funding Agency
This organisation funds and regulates adult further education and skills training in England. The organisation aims to ensure that people and businesses can access the skills training they need.
www.skillsfundingagency.bis.gov.uk

Organisations involved specifically in the management of complaints and appeals

EAB (Examinations Appeals Board)
This organisation manages the final stage of appeals for GCSE and A-level examinations.
www.theeab.org.uk

Office for the Independent Adjudicator
This body is responsible for managing complaints and appeals made by students in higher education.
www.oiahe.org.uk

Organisations involved in funding qualifications
These organisations provide advice and support, and they process applications for funding.

Educational Grants Service (EGS)
Provides information and advice on the funding available in post-16 education and training. This service is available through the family action website.
www.family-action.org.uk

Higher Education Funding Council for England (HEFCE)
This body promotes and funds teaching and research in England.
www.hefce.ac.uk

Higher Education Funding Council for Wales (HEFCW)
This body promotes and funds teaching and research in Wales.
www.hefcw.ac.uk

Scottish Funding Council
This body promotes and funds teaching, learning and research in Scotland.
www.sfc.ac.uk

Student Awards Agency Scotland
Gives advice and support to students based in Scotland applying for higher education. This organisation also processes applications for funding.
www.saas.gov.uk

Student Finance England
Gives advice and support to students based in England applying for higher education. This organisation also processes applications for funding. This service is powered through the Directgov service.
www.direct.gov.uk

Student Finance NI
Gives advice and support to students based in Northern Ireland applying for higher education. This organisation also processes applications for funding.
www.studentfinanceni.co.uk

Student Finance Wales
Gives advice and support to students based in Wales applying for higher education. This organisation also processes applications for funding.
www.studentfinancewales.co.uk

Student Finance Services European Team
This unit at the Student Loans Company provides information to EU students on student finance in the UK.

Young Person's Learning Agency (will be replaced by the Education Funding Agency in 2012)
This organisation champions education and training for young people in England, with a specific remit to fund academies, provide financial support to young learners and assure suitable education and training is available for young people.
www.ypla.gov.uk

Adult Funding
For information on adult funding in Wales visit the *Adult Guide to Funding* through the Welsh Assembly Government website. The *myworldofwork* website hosted by Skills Development Scotland provides information on adult funding in Scotland. The *Help with Learning Costs* section of the nidirect government website provides information about adult funding in Northern Ireland. The *Education and Learning* section of the Directgov website provides information on adult funding in England.

Organisations involved in the development of skills

The following organisations promote and support skills development in the UK.

Alliance of Sector Skills Councils
This body acts as a single voice for sector skills councils working across the UK and retains an up-to-date list of the current sector skills councils in the UK.
www.sscalliance.org

BBC Skillswise
The BBC Skillswise website has a range of tools and games promoting literacy and numeracy skills.
www.bbc.co.uk/skillswise

Move On
This service provides a range of information and tools promoting the development of literacy and numeracy.
www.move-on.org.uk

Skills Development Scotland
This organisation is responsible for promoting and developing skills across Scotland.
www.skillsdevelopmentscotland.co.uk

The Big Plus
Managed by Skills Development Scotland this service provides a helpline and a range of resources supporting reading, writing and numeracy skills for learners in Scotland.
www.thebigplus.com

Where to search for qualifications, learning providers and get careers advice

Government services

Careers Service Northern Ireland
This organisation provides careers advice to learners across Northern Ireland.
www.careersserviceni.com

Careers Wales
The careerswales website provides advice and allows you to search for over 30,000 courses in learning providers across Wales.
www.careerswales.com

Directgov
Directgov provides details of nearly 900,000 courses in the UK. It also provides information on how the qualification system works, funding and other benefits.
www.direct.gov.uk

Edubase
Powered by the Department of Education this search engine allows you to search for learning providers across England and Wales.
www.edubase.gov.uk

Jobcentre Plus
This service provides tools and support helping people back into work.
www.direct.gov.uk

Local Councils
Local Councils provide comprehensive information on education provision in your area. The Directgov service provides a Local Council finder.
www.direct.gov.uk

Next Step Careers Service
This service provides careers advice for adults.
www.nextstep.direct.gov.uk
Please note that young learners between the ages of 13-19 should go to the *Information, Advice and Support for Young People* section of the Directgov website.

NIdirect
The Nidirect website in Northern Ireland uses many of the search facilities of Directgov but is customised to meet the specific educational requirements in Northern Ireland.
www.nidirect.gov.uk

Opendays.com
A directory of open days in universities and colleges across the UK.
www.opendays.com

Prospects
This is the UK's official graduate website, enabling you to search for postgraduate jobs and courses and get careers advice.
www.prospects.ac.uk

SQA
This website provides a search engine for qualifications outside of higher education.
www.sqa.org.uk

myworldofwork
This website enables you to run detailed searches for qualifications in Scotland and also provides a range of tools and services supporting career development.
www.myworldofwork.skillsdevelopmentscotland.co.uk

The Register of Regulated Qualifications
This register lists regulated vocational and 14-19 qualifications offered across England, Wales and Northern Ireland.
www.register.ofqual.gov.uk

UCAS(Universities and Colleges and Admissions Service)
This service provides a directory of higher education qualifications available at universities and colleges across the UK. It also provides detailed profiles of those universities and colleges.
www.ucas.com

UKPASS (UK Postgraduate Application and Statistical Service)
This service provides a search engine for postgraduate qualifications.
www.ukpass.com

UK Register of Learning Providers (UKRLP)
This register lists information on learning providers across the UK.
www.ukrlp.co.uk

Unistats
The official website providing statistics on universities in the UK including the results of the latest National Student Survey.
www.unistats.gov.uk

Private organisations

Bestcourse4me.com
This service enables you to assess the benefits of taking a particular qualification by showing you the link between what people have studied and their career record afterwards.
www.bestcourse4me.com

Floodlight
Floodlight was originally set up to promote adult learning in London. It has since expanded and now provides a comprehensive guide to courses available nationally. The Floodlight service enables you to search by subject, local area, type of learning, by most popular courses, and by local college. Floodlight provides different websites for regions and cities. From each website there are links to other regions so a good place to start is the London website.
www.london.floodlight.co.uk

Hotcourses
The UK's biggest search engine for courses, providing consumer ratings on courses and learning providers.
www.hotcourses.com

Learndirect
This is the UK's biggest provider of online qualifications.
www.learndirect.co.uk

Push
Provides an independent guide to UK universities and a range of other tools and services.
www.push.co.uk

Whatuni.com
Provides a search engine for universities and independent consumer ratings of courses and learning providers.
www.whatuni.com

Representative bodies

National Union of Students
This body campaigns on behalf of students and provides a range of discounts, tools and services to student members.
www.nus.org.uk

Russell Group
This body represents 20 leading universities in the UK.
www.russellgroup.ac.uk

Help and advice for international students
The following organisations provide information and advice to students wanting to study in the UK.

British Council
The *educationuk* website provides detailed information for international students on education and life in the UK.
www.educationuk.org

British Council
The *prepare for success* website is a learning hub providing a range of activities designed to develop the skills needed to study in the UK.
www.prepareforsuccess.org.uk

GostudyUK
Provides an informal source of information and advice to international students.
www.gostudyuk.com

QS Top Universities
QS provides international links between graduates and business schools, postgraduate departments at universities and employers worldwide. QS provides a range of tools and country profiles to support graduates selecting postgraduate courses.
www.topuniversities.com

UK Council for International Student Affairs (UKCISA)
This organisation provides a range of services and information for international students studying in the UK.
www.ukcisa.org.uk

UK NARIC
The National Recognition Information Centre for the UK provides official information on how UK qualifications compare to international qualifications in over 180 countries.
www.naric.org.uk

European information services and initiatives
The following organisations and services support learners across Europe.

Erasmus Programme
The European Regional Action Scheme for the Mobility of University Students allows European students to study and work in another European country.
www.ec.europa.eu.

EURES – The European Job Mobility Portal
An online hub of information and resources supporting working across the European Union.
www.eures.europa.eu

Europass
A common template for developing your Curriculum Vitae which is accepted by organisations across the European Union.
www.europass.cedefop.europa.eu

European Commission – Your Europe website
The Education and Youth section provides advice about schools, universities and traineeships by EU member state.
www.ec.europa.eu/youreurope

Leonardo Programme
An EU initiative supporting exchange programmes for learners studying vocational qualifications.
www.ec.europa.eu

Qualifications can cross boundaries – a rough guide to comparing qualifications in UK and Ireland
This tool enables you to compare different qualifications sitting across different qualification frameworks in the UK and Ireland.
www.nqai.ie/docs/publications/UK_comparison_guide.pdf

Services supporting disabled learners

AbilityNet
A UK charity providing support on the use of technology for disabled adults and children.
www.abilitynet.org.uk

Capability Scotland
This organisation provides advice and support to disabled learners in Scotland.
www.capability-scotland.org.uk

Directgov
Provides information about rights and funding for disabled learners and represents a good starting point for a search for further information.
www.direct.gov.uk

Disability Alliance
This organisation provides information, resources and a confidential helpline for disabled learners through the skills section of its website.
www.disablityalliance.org

Foundation for People with Learning Disabilities
This organisation uses research and projects to promote the rights and opportunities of people with learning disabilities.
www.learningdisablities.org.uk

Lead Scotland
An organisation committed to widening access to education and training for disabled learners.
www.lead.org.uk

Organisations responsible for the processing of student applications

UCAS (Universities and Colleges Admissions Service)
This service centrally manages applications to universities and other institutes of higher education.
www.ucas.com

UKPASS (UK Postgraduate Application and Statistical Service)
This service centrally manages some postgraduate applications on behalf of institutes of higher education.
www.ukpass.com

Glossary

0-9

14-19 qualifications Publicly funded qualifications, typically taken by young people between the ages of 14 and 19, which determine entry into further and higher education or employment.

A

Access arrangements The steps taken to enable a learner to participate fully in the assessment of a qualification. See also 'reasonable adjustments'.

Accreditation The scrutiny and subsequent recognition of qualifications and learning providers by an external organisation.

Accreditation of prior learning The process of identifying and validating the knowledge and skills gained by a learner prior to starting a course. This can lead to exemptions from units in that course.

Admissions process The system and procedures used by learning providers to select appropriate candidates for a qualification.

Admissions tutor The person responsible for reviewing whether an applicant meets the entry requirements for a qualification.

Adult learning/education Courses and qualifications taken by adults, often involving re-entry into the education system. This term is used interchangeably with lifelong learning.

Anonymous marking Assessed work which does not reveal the identity of the candidate in order to minimise bias in the marking of that work.

Appeal	When a learner, or learning provider representing a learner, challenges the result they have gained in an assessment and requests a remark.
Appeals board	A group of examiners/assessors responsible for reviewing the results of assessments challenged by a learner.
Application procedures	The tasks which need to be completed in applying for a qualification at a particular learning provider.
Applied learning	Acquiring and applying knowledge and skills in the workplace or a context similar to work.
Assessment	The process of making a judgement about the extent to which a learner's work meets the assessment criteria for a unit or qualification.
Assessment criteria	The requirements that learners need to fulfil to demonstrate they have acquired the necessary knowledge and skills in a unit or qualification.
Assessor	The person responsible for making a judgement on a learner's work.
Authentication	Confirmation that the work is original to the learner and has been produced to the required standard.
Award	The term is used interchangeably with qualification and certificate and is used to describe the end point when you successfully gain the qualification.
Awarding organisation	An organisation recognised by the qualification regulators in the UK for the purposes of developing and awarding qualifications. These are also described as exam boards.

B

Blended learning	Learning conducted in a number of different ways.
Board of examiners	A group of subject experts responsible for checking the quality of marking in a qualification.

Bursary	This is an amount of money towards the cost of qualification which does not need to be paid back. A bursary is usually offered by the learning provider.

C

Careers adviser	A trained professional who is able to provided impartial advice on the career and training opportunities available to a learner.
Certificate	The formal record documenting the achievement of a qualification.
Cohort	A group of learners who study together on the same course.
Complaints procedure	How to make a complaint about any aspect of a qualification or learning provider.
Compulsory units	The parts of a qualification that must be achieved in order to complete that qualification. This term is used interchangeably with mandatory or core units.
Controlled assessment	This type of assessment allows you to produce a piece of work over a period of time; however this work must be produced under supervision and cannot be taken home.
Course	This describes structured learning over a period of time, characterised by some form of attendance and assessment. Not all courses lead to recognised qualifications.
Course fees	This is the main fee paid when a learner takes a qualification. This covers the cost of the teaching, resources and facilities and for certain qualifications it is paid on behalf of the learner by the government. The terms 'tuition fees' and 'course fees' are interchangeable.
Coursework	Assessed work with a given date for submission which can be completed by the learner in their own time and outside of their place of study.

Credit	A measurement used to describe the size of units and qualifications. It is also defined as the award a learner gains by successfully completing the learning outcomes in a particular unit.
Credit accumulation	The process of gaining credit over time through the successful completion of units of study.
Credit transfer	Schemes recognised between learning providers that allow learners to build up and move credit between different units, qualifications and providers.
Customer charter	A document which outlines the customer service levels learners can expect from an organisation.

D

Data security	In this context, ensuring appropriate steps have been taken to safeguard learner data, results information and assessments.
Degree awarding powers	The right of a learning provider to award degrees, which is granted by the Privy Council or by Royal Charter, on the basis of recommendations from the Quality Assurance Agency.
Diagnostic assessment	An assessment of the learner's knowledge and skills at the start of a course.
Discretionary support fund	Funds for low-income learners which are allocated by the learning provider, such as a school or college.
Distance learning	A course which does not require the learner to have face-to- face contact with their teacher. This type of course is often delivered via internet, CD-Rom or through paper-based correspondence.
Double marking	A means of ensuring the accuracy of marking assessments by getting two independent markers to separately mark the same assessment.

E

Economic regulation — A new approach by qualification regulators focused on ensuring prices for qualifications are fair and transparent.

Education authorities — The agencies, regulators and inspectorates working across the UK who have the responsibility for safeguarding the quality of qualifications and teaching.

Education loans — An amount of money which needs to be paid back over a period of time.

Employability — The role of a qualification in developing the knowledge and skills required for the workplace.

Employer recognition — A government scheme designed to recognise formally the training provided by employers.

Enquiry about a result (EAR) — This is a request for an assessment to be remarked which is usually made by a learning provider representing a learner.

Entry requirements — The qualifications and experience learners are required to demonstrate to gain entry onto a course.

Examination — An assessment of a learner's knowledge and skills usually in a formal setting under supervised conditions.

Examination fees — The fee learners are typically charged for sitting the examination at the end of each unit or module. This fee may be in addition to the tuition fees they pay.

Exemptions — When a learner is not required to take a particular unit because of the knowledge and skills they have previously gained elsewhere.

External assessment — As used outside higher education, when the marking of assessed work is the responsibility of the qualification developer and not the learning provider that teaches the qualification.

External assessor or examiner — An independent expert who is not known to the learner, responsible for marking assessments or reviewing the quality of marking.

External verifier	An independent expert who is responsible for reviewing the quality of marking.

F

Formal learning	Structured learning which is supervised in some way.
Formative assessment	Assessments used to review the progress made by learners during their course of study.
Free qualification	A qualification in which all, or the main, fees are paid by the government. This is often dependent on the type of learner taking that qualification.
Further education	Post-compulsory education, prior to degree-level education (higher education).

G

Grades	A scale used to differentiate levels of achievement at the end of a unit or qualification.
Grade boundaries	The mark, often expressed in percentage form, which differentiates levels of achievement.
Grant	An amount of money paid towards the cost of a qualification that does not need to be paid back.
Guided learning hours (GLH)	A measurement of the time spent learning under the supervision of a teacher or coordinator. This measurement does not encompass the time given to private study.

H

Higher education (HE)	The stage of learning that takes place at universities and other higher education institutions that award degrees or equivalent certificates.
Higher education institutions	Universities and colleges which offer recognised qualifications in the Framework for Higher Education Qualifications (FHEQ), such as bachelors and masters degrees.

Higher level qualification	Qualifications which are positioned at a higher, and therefore more difficult level, within a particular qualification framework.
Home students	Those students that are residents of the country in which the course is offered.

I

Informal learning	Learning that is not organised but occurs as part of daily experience.
Inspectorates	Organisations with a responsibility to review the quality of learning providers in areas such as the quality of teaching, resources and management.
Internal assessment	As used outside higher education, a form of assessment in which the learning provider marks the assessments. This marking is then quality assured by the qualification developer.
Internal assessor/examiner	A person working for the learning provider who is responsible for marking assessments, often the teacher of the relevant subject.
Internal verifier	A person appointed by the learning provider to review the quality of marking.
Invigilator	A person appointed to supervise an examination and ensure that exam rules are followed.

L

Lead verifier	The person with an overall responsibility for the quality of marking for a particular qualification.
Lecture	A form of teaching that involves a presentation to a large number of students.
Learning outcomes	What you are expected to know, understand or be able to do as a consequence of your learning.
Learning providers	Organisations responsible for delivering a qualification to learners, including schools, colleges, universities, employers, prisons and a wide variety of other providers.
Level	A way of grouping qualifications according to their difficulty.

Level indicators/descriptors	Statements outlining what knowledge and skills you need to demonstrate at each level.
Lifelong learning	The courses and qualifications taken by adults, often involving re-entry into the education system. This term is used interchangeably with adult learning.
Listed body	An organisation recognised by a university and by the UK government as having sufficient expertise to develop and deliver modules of a higher education programme.
Local authority	This term is used to describe the local government in a particular area and is used interchangeably with local council. Local authorities have a range of responsibilities in education including the distribution of funding for state schools and coordinating the allocation of places available in each state school. They are also a comprehensive source of information about education and training in that area.

M

Maladministration	An act of negligence which impacts on the delivery of a qualification.
Malpractice	A deliberate act of wrongdoing which impacts on the delivery of a qualification.
Mock examinations	An opportunity given to learners to practise taking assessments in supervised conditions.
Moderation	The process of cross checking the quality of marking. This can often involve a second person marking a sample of work.
Modules	The distinct blocks of learning that make up a qualification. This term is used interchangeably with units.

N

National occupational standards	The skills recognised as required to do a job competently in a particular sector such as engineering.

National recognition	Signalling that a qualification has been approved by the education authorities as meeting the required standard.
Nominal learning hours	A measurement which includes both the supervised learning and private study time required to complete units and qualifications.
Non-formal learning	The learning gained at work or in other environments.

O

Optional units	Units a learner can select in addition to the compulsory units they are required to study.
Open days	Days when the public are invited to visit a learning provider and explore the facilities. Student guides are often provided to give further information.

P

Pass rates	The percentage of learners on a course who successfully meet the required standard.
Pastoral support	The support given by a learning provider outside of the teaching of a subject. This support can address managing personal problems, administrative issues, complaints and questions about future plans.
Performance tables	Published rankings given to qualifications and learning providers against defined criteria.
Performance points	A value given to many qualifications taken by 14-19 year olds on the basis of size and difficulty.
Personal tutor	A teacher responsible for supporting students on non-academic issues. This system is commonly used in universities.
Plagiarism	A form of cheating involving falsely claiming ownership of work copied from other sources.
Practice papers	Questions and tasks given to learners in preparation for their formal assessment.

Prior achievement	Previous recognised learning gained from units, qualifications or the workplace.
Private tuition	A situation where the learner pays a tutor directly for one-to-one teaching in a particular subject.
Professional bodies/ organisations	Organisations, including chartered institutes and royal institutes, which are responsible for the development and teaching of qualifications enabling access or advancement in a particular profession.
Professional career development loan	A bank loan supporting vocational or work-related learning. The interest is paid by the government for the duration of the qualification and for one month after.
Professional qualifications	A broad term commonly used to describe those qualifications which enable entry or advancement in an occupation.
Progression	The process of moving from one qualification to another at a higher level.
Prospectus	The marketing material promoting a particular qualification or learning provider.
Publicly funded qualifications	Qualifications which have been specifically approved by governments in the UK as eligible for government funding.

Q

Qualification	A course of study developing knowledge and skills for a particular purpose. A learner is typically assessed in some form at the end of each unit. If successful in achieving the required standard the learner will be awarded a certificate.
Qualification delivery	A broad term which encompasses the variety of different ways you can study a qualification and the range of different places in which learning can take place.

Qualification developer	The organisation which designs and awards the qualification. It determines the content and level of the qualification and how it will be assessed.
Qualification framework	A system for organising qualifications by levels. The levels start at entry level or level 1 and go up. The higher the level, the more difficult the qualification.
Qualification regulators	Organisations responsible for safeguarding your rights as learner when taking a regulated qualification.
Quality assurance	The process of scrutinising the quality of a qualification.

R

Recognition of prior achievement	The process of identifying and validating the knowledge and skills held by a learner prior to starting a course. This can lead to exemptions from units in that course.
Registration fee	A fee charged for registering for a qualification, in addition to the tuition fee. This is an administrative fee covering the costs of registration.
Regulated qualifications	Qualifications that have been scrutinised by the education authorities and are recognised as meeting the required standard.
Replacement fees	The charge a learner is required to pay if they lose their certificate and ask for a copy to be produced.
Research assessment evaluation rating (RAE rating)	The judgements made on the quality of research in higher education by the research funding bodies in the UK.
Reasonable adjustments	The measures taken to ensure disabled learners are not unfairly disadvantaged when taking a qualification.
Resit	An opportunity to retake a unit or the whole qualification.
Results	The information provided to learners on their level of achievement at the end of a unit or qualification.

S

Scholarships — These provide an amount of money which you do not pay back. They are given by learning providers and many other private organisations and are designed to support learners with excellent academic records and/or in difficult financial circumstances.

Seminars — A way of delivering teaching in a small group fostering discussions between a teacher and learners.

Special considerations — Measures taken in managing a learner whose exam performance has been affected by adverse circumstances such as illness, injury or family bereavement.

Sponsorship — Contributions to the cost of a qualification made by an employer or another organisation. This can be contingent on joining or continuing to work for that employer.

Standard — This term describes the difficulty of a qualification. The standard of a particular qualification should be the same regardless of where it is taught in the country and which organisation is delivering it to you.

Standardisation — A process which aims to ensure that assessors have sufficient knowledge of the assessment criteria to mark assessments effectively. For example, assessors might be asked to mark a number of past or dummy scripts and then review the marks given.

Student handbook — A practical guide giving information to learners. This usually outlines the services and support available and lays down the rights and responsibilities of learners.

Student welfare — The service within a learning provider, designed to provide advice and support to learners.

Summative assessment — The formal assessment of a learner's knowledge and skills at the end of a unit or qualification.

T

Taster sessions — Classes designed to give new learners an experience of how a particular subject will be taught.

Training — Learning that happens both inside and outside of a qualification. This term often refers to the development of the skills in the workplace.

Transcript — A formal document, produced in addition to a certificate, providing a more detailed breakdown of the marks awarded.

Tuition fees — The main fee paid when a learner takes a qualification. The terms 'tuition fees' and 'course fees' are interchangeable. This fee covers the money spent on the teaching, resources and facilities by the organisation delivering the qualification and for certain qualifications is paid on behalf of the learner by the government.

U

Unique learner number (ULN) — A system which identifies learners with a unique number that is used to register personal information and to track and manage results.

Units — The distinct blocks of learning that make up a qualification. This term is used interchangeably with modules.

Universities and Colleges Admissions Service (UCAS) Tariff — This is a point system used by universities to compare the different qualifications enabling entry to undergraduate courses in higher education.

V

Vocational qualifications — Qualifications which enable learners to develop and apply the skills needed in the workplace.

W

Work-based learning — The knowledge and skills developed in the workplace.

Index

0-9

14-19 Diploma 168
14-19 Qualifications 34, 51, 55, 74, 165

A

A level 33, 52, 77, 155, 165
Abilitynet 122, 187
Academies 33, 159
Access arrangements for disabled learners 101
Accommodation 51, 53, 92, 99, 111, 136
Accreditation 65-66, 177
Accreditation of prior learning 16
Additional time 137
Admission process 88-89
Admissions tutor 9, 17, 66, 67
Adult funding 54, 180
Adult learning 34-35, 54, 161
Adult literacy 52, 67, 79, 119, 138, 162, 168
Adult numeracy 19, 35, 67-68, 162
Advanced highers 167
Advice 4, 117
Alliance of Sector Skills Councils 132, 180
Anonymous marking 81
Appeals 84, 135, 145, 178
Application procedures 88-90, 111
Applied learning 21
Apprenticeships 67, 170
AS level 165
Assessment 4, 12, 18-20, 22, 28, 73, 75-76, 82

Assessment criteria 19, 72-74
Assessor 19-20, 104
Authentication 19
Award 22
Awarding organisation 28, 36, 60, 75, 80

B

Bachelor's degree 13, 53, 65, 74, 154, 172
BBC Skillwise website 120, 181
Bestcourse4me.com 67, 184
Bias 81
Blended learning 116
Board of examiners 145
Bridge Schools Inspectorate (BSI) 177
British Accreditation Council 66, 177
British Council 89, 121, 142
    Accreditation UK 66, 177
    Prepare for Success website 121, 185
BTEC 75, 153-155, 171
Bursary 50-53

C

Cambridge Pre-U 165
Capability Scotland 122, 187
Careers adviser 117-118, 67
Careers Service Northern Ireland 117, 181
Careers Wales 115, 118, 181
CCEA (Council for Curriculum Examinations and Assessment) 65, 176

Certificate 11, 22, 47, 61-62, 136, 146-147
Cheating 82
Class sizes 95, 111
Cohort 146
Complaints 84, 102, 135-136, 146, 148
Complaints procedures 103, 136-137
Comprehensive schools 33, 159
Compulsory units 11
Computer centre 92, 94, 139
Concessions 45, 61
Conditional offer 41
Consumer feedback 107, 110
Continuously assessed 19, 21
Controlled conditions 77
Core skills 168
Correspondence learning 163
Cost 3, 44, 48-49, 50-51, 53, 60, 68
Course 22, 61
Course fees 45, 51, 61
Coursework 77
Credit 15-18
Credit and qualifications framework for Wales (CQFW) 152
Credit transfer 16
Customer charter 103
Customer service 31, 84, 102, 111

D

Data security 31, 104, 136, 146
Degree awarding powers 29
Department for Business Innovation and Skills (BIS) 51, 175
Department for Education 109, 116, 175
Department for Education in Northern Ireland 116, 175
Destination survey 94
Diagnostic assessment 20
Differentiation 79

Directgov 55, 114, 118, 121, 140, 181, 187
Discrimination 83, 135, 139
Disability adviser 139
Disabled learner 54, 56, 100-101, 111, 121
Disability Alliance 122, 140, 187
Discretionary support fund 50, 55
Distance learning 162, 170, 172
Distance learning providers 162
Doctorate (PhD) 20, 153, 173-174
Double marking 81
Dyslexia 137

E

EAB (Examinations Appeal Board) 178
Economic regulation 141
Edubase 116, 182
Education allowances 51
Education authorities 9, 27-28, 30, 49, 62
Educational Grants Service (EQS) 179
Education loans 51, 53-54
Education maintenance allowance 55
Education Scotland 177
Education UK website 121, 185
Employability 66-67
Employers 9, 17, 29, 34, 59, 66-67, 162
Employer recognition 17
ENIC NARIC 126
English for speakers of other languages (ESOL) 156
Enquiry about a result (EAR) 84
Enrolment 88
Entry requirements 76, 88, 111, 115, 121
Erasmus programme 124, 186
Essential Skills Northern Ireland 169
Essential Skills Wales 169

ESTYN 66, 177
ETINI 66, 177
EURES – The European Job Mobility Portal 129-130, 186
Europass 129-130, 186
European Commission's Compare Qualifications Frameworks interactive tool 127
European Commission – Your Europe website 129, 186
European Credit Transfer Scheme (ECTS) 129
European Higher Education Area (EHEA) 124
European Qualifications Framework (EQF) 62, 124-127, 130
EU student 46, 50, 54
Examination 75-78, 80, 82
Examination fees 47, 140
Exclusions 160
Exemptions 17
External assessment 19
External assessor or examiner 19-20, 36, 81
External verifier 81
Extracurricular activities 91

F

Faith schools 160
Feedback 79, 99
Flexibility 11, 16-17, 22, 60, 163, 172
Floodlight 184
Formal learning 23
Formative assessment 20
Foundation degrees 170
Foundation for People with Learning Disabilities 122, 187
Framework for Higher Education Qualifications (FHEQ) 151-153
Free qualification 52
Free schools 160
French Baccalaureate 27

Fresher fairs 91
Further education (FE) 34, 41, 161
Further education college 34, 52, 54, 60, 105, 138, 161
Functional skills 156-157, 169
Funding 27, 50, 54, 178

G

GCSEs 33, 52, 77, 137, 156, 166
General qualifications 33
GostudyUK website 121, 185
Grades 20, 41, 61, 73, 75
Grade boundaries 20
Grammar schools 160
Grant 50, 53-55
Guided learning hours (GLH) 14-15

H

Higher education (HE) 29, 34, 41, 51, 54, 65, 161
Higher education fairs 98
Higher education institutions 31, 34, 65, 161
Higher Education Funding Council for England (HEFCE) 179
Higher Education Funding Council for Wales (HEFCW) 179
Higher education maintenance grant 53
Higher level qualification 15, 38, 40
Higher national certificates (HNCs) 117, 154, 171
Higher national diplomas (HNDs) 171, 154
Home school 45, 159
Home study 36, 163
Home students 45
Hotcourses website 107, 111, 184

I

IELTS 74, 142

IGCSEs 166
Independent schools 160
Informal learning 17, 23
Information 4, 58-59, 72, 74, 90, 111, 114, 117
Inspectorates 134, 177
Inspection reports 105, 110
Internal assessment 19
Internal verifier 81
International students 46, 50, 54, 121, 185
Invigilator 19, 47
Independent Schools Inspectorate (ISI) 66, 178

J

Jobcentre Plus 119, 182

K

Key skills 169

L

Lead Scotland 122, 188
Lead Verifier 145
Lecture 95
Learndirect Service 115-116, 120, 184
Leonardo Programme 129, 187
Learning environment 94, 96, 135, 138
Learning outcomes 12-13, 19, 61, 72-73
Learning providers 4, 32, 33, 54, 91, 98, 111, 134
Learning style 3, 21
Level 3, 39-41, 59, 64, 68, 152-154
Level indicators/descriptors 42
Library 48, 95
Lifelong learning 34, 161
Listed body 29
Local authorities 27, 116-117, 182
Local test centres 162

M

Maladministration 103
Malpractice 103
Marking 79-80
Marking scheme 74, 80-81
Master's degree 12, 65, 74, 153, 173
Middle schools 159
Mock examinations 77
Moderation 81
Modules 10, 13, 29, 36, 59
Move On Service 119, 181
Multiple choice assessment 20
Myworldofwork website 55, 115, 118, 183

N

National curriculum 33, 170
Nationally recognised qualifications 17, 20, 32, 40, 62
National occupational standards 32, 171
National qualifications framework (NQF) 125, 152-153
National student survey 108
National Union of Students 48, 185
Next Step Careers Service 52-53, 55, 118, 182
Nidirect 55, 114, 182
Nominal learning hours 114-115
Non-formal learning 23
NVQs (National vocational qualifications) 155-156, 172

O

Office for the Independent Adjudicator 145, 178
Ofsted (Office for Standards in Education, Children's Services and Skills) 66, 105-106, 178
Ofqual (Office of Qualifications and Examinations Regulation) 65, 176

Online learning providers 44, 162
Open days 97, 111
Opendays.com 97, 182
Open University 36
Optional units 12

P

Pass rates 75, 94
Pastoral support 98, 111, 137
Peer assessment 74
Peer observations 100
Performance tables 108, 110
Performance points 34, 109
Personal tutors 137
Plagiarism 78, 82
Postgraduate certificates 153, 172
Postgraduate diplomas 153, 172
Practice papers 80
Price See cost
Primary education 33, 159
Prior achievement 16
Prisons 162
Private providers 163
Private schools 160
Private tuition 22
Professional and career development loan 53
Professional organisations 29
Progression 38, 59
Prospectus 93, 110-111
Prospects 115, 182
Publicly funded qualifications 52
Pupil referral units 160
Push website 107, 184

Q

QS TopUniversities service 185
Qualification 1, 4, 8, 9, 14, 22, 26, 39, 58
Qualification consumer 2, 5, 21, 77-78, 133
Qualification delivery 34
Qualification developers 27, 31, 33, 49, 60-61, 78, 134
Qualification length 14, 60, 68
Qualification regulator 9, 62-63, 65, 137, 176
Qualifications and credit framework (QCF) 15, 17, 29, 152-153
'Qualifications can cross boundaries' 125, 187
Qualifications framework 31, 38, 40, 42, 59, 151
Qualifications framework for the European Higher Education Area 124
Qualification specification 75
Quality assurance 30, 62, 69, 75, 78, 176
Quality Assurance Agency (QAA) 31, 66, 105, 107-108, 111

R

Rational consumer 13, 18, 49, 120, 150
Reasonable adjustments 20-21, 75, 83, 100, 139
Recognition of prior achievement 16
Refund 47, 139, 142
Register of Regulated Qualifications 115, 183
Registration fees 47
Regulated qualifications 63-64, 69
Reliability 135
Re-mark 84, 135
Replacement fees 47
Reputation 3, 9-10, 58, 66-67, 69
Research assessment evaluation (RAE) rating 107
Resit 76, 146
Results 61-62, 75, 77, 79
Russell Group 108, 185

S

Scholarships 51, 53
School Inspection Service (SIS) 178
School sixth forms 161
Scottish credit and qualifications framework (SCQF) 125
Scottish Funding Council 179
Scottish government 109, 175
Scottish Highers 77, 166
Scottish qualification certificates 33
Secondary education 33, 159
Sector skills councils 32, 59, 66, 92
Self assessment 74
Seminars 95
Sixth form colleges 105, 161
Skills Development Scotland 55, 115, 120
Skills for life qualifications 120, 170
Skills Funding Agency 52, 138, 178
Special considerations 21, 75, 82
Special requirements 20, 139
Special schools 160
Sponsorship 51
SQA 114
SQA Accreditation 65, 176
Standard 9, 134
Standardisation 81
Standard grades (Scottish qualification) 167
State schools 33
Student Awards Agency Scotland 54, 179
Student Finance England 54, 179
Student Finance NI 54, 179
Student Finance Services European Team 54, 180
Student Finance Wales 54, 80
Student handbook 93, 111
Student profile 94
Student room 96, 111
Student staff liaison committees 98
Student surveys 96, 99, 110
Student welfare 32, 42, 111
Summative assessment 20
SVQs (Scottish Vocational Qualifications) 17

T

Taster sessions 97
Teaching 98, 100, 111, 134
The Big Plus website 120, 181
Titles 13, 41, 59, 61
Training 23
Transcript 62
Transparency 81, 101, 103
Tuition fees 45-46, 51, 53

U

UCAS (Universities and Colleges Admissions Service) 53-54, 89, 97, 115, 183, 188
UCAS Tariff 40-41
UK Council for International Student Affairs (UKCISA) 121, 129
UK NARIC (National Recognition Information Centre for the UK) 89, 121, 126, 186
UKPASS (UK Postgraduate Application and Statistical Service) 89, 183, 188
UK Register of Learning Providers (UKRLP) 116, 183
Unique learner number (ULN) 105, 61
Unistats 108, 111, 183
Units 10-11, 44, 59
University 26, 28, 31, 53, 162
Unregulated qualifications 64

V

Visa requirements 89, 92
Vocational qualifications 10, 18, 33-34, 53, 59, 74, 83

W

Welsh Assembly government 54, 65, 176
Welsh Baccalaureate 33, 167
Whatuni.com website 107, 111, 184
Wheelchair access 102
Witness statements 83
Wolf report 34, 109
Work based learning 36, 162

Y

Young Person's Learning Agency (To be replaced by the Education Funding Agency) 52, 180

About the author

Toby Higson is a leading authority on the UK qualifications system. He advises organisations across the private and public sectors, from small private colleges through to international qualification developers and government agencies. Much of his current work is focused on improving the quality of the qualifications, the resources and the services that are offered to learners, and on achieving alignment with regulation and best practice.

Acknowledgements

I would like to thank my friends and family for all of their support as I wrote this book. Particular thanks go to the editorial team at Rivington for all their work in shaping the book and bringing it into existence.

Toby Higson, 2011